Disney's Kilala Princess

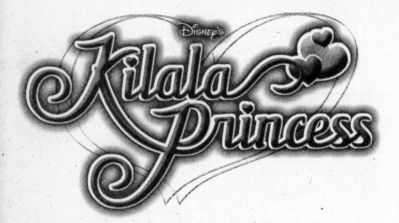

Volume 1

Art by Nao Kodaka
Story by Rika Tanaka

TOKYOPOP

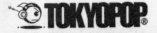

HAMBURG // LONDON // LOS ANGELES // TOKYO

Contents

Chapter 1......5

Chapter 2.....56

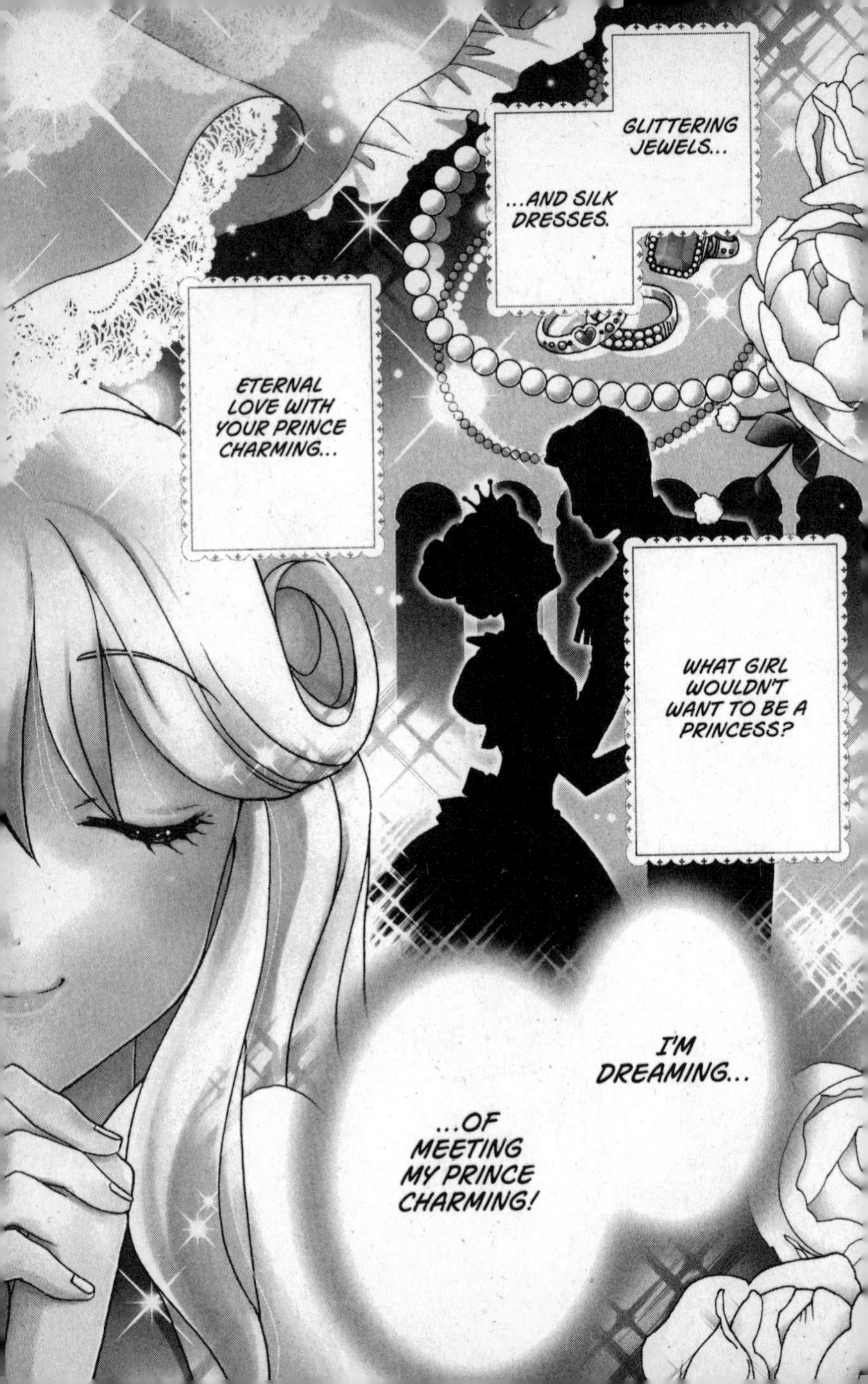
GLITTERING JEWELS...
...AND SILK DRESSES.
ETERNAL LOVE WITH YOUR PRINCE CHARMING...
WHAT GIRL WOULDN'T WANT TO BE A PRINCESS?
I'M DREAMING...
...OF MEETING MY PRINCE CHARMING!

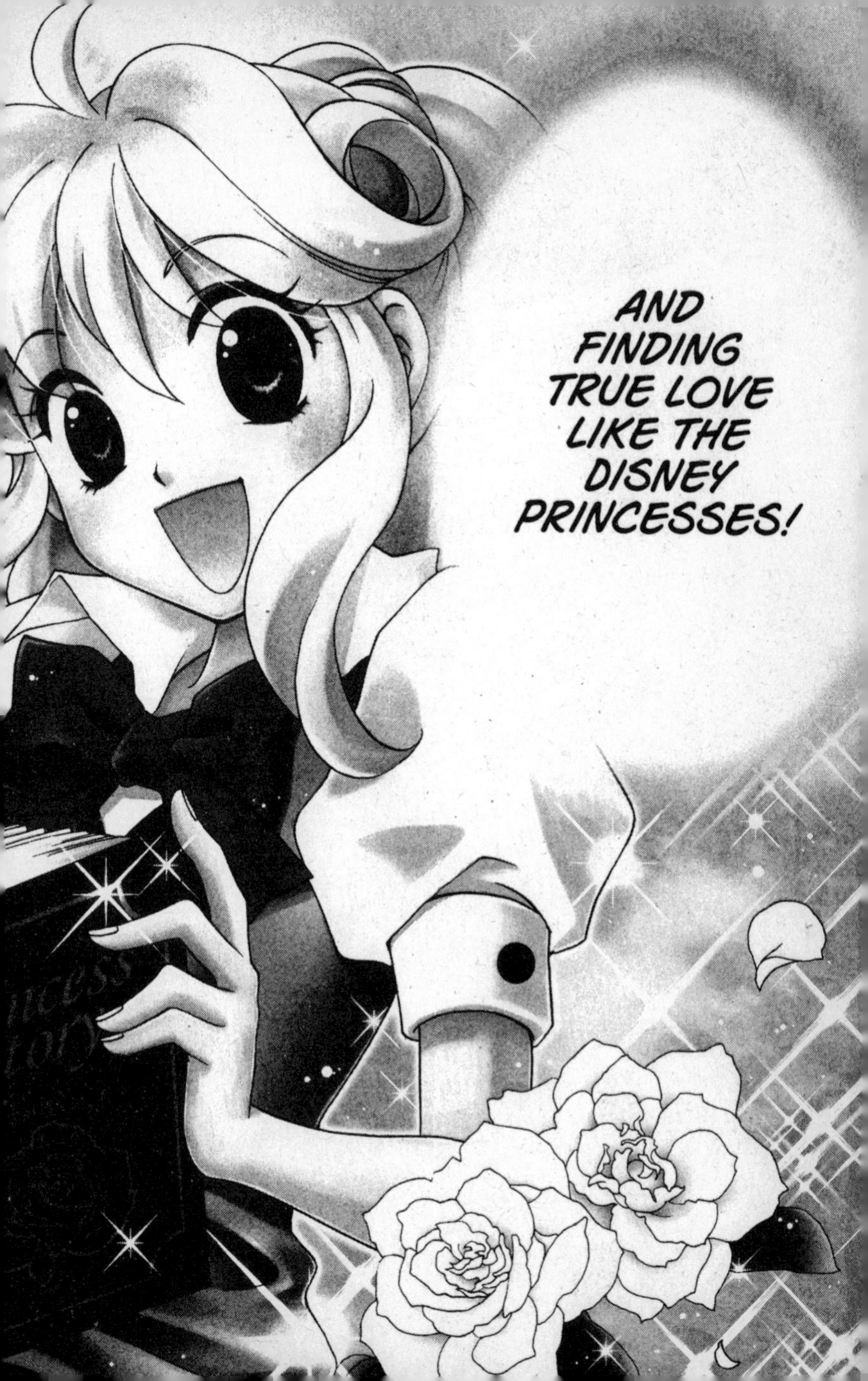
AND FINDING TRUE LOVE LIKE THE DISNEY PRINCESSES!

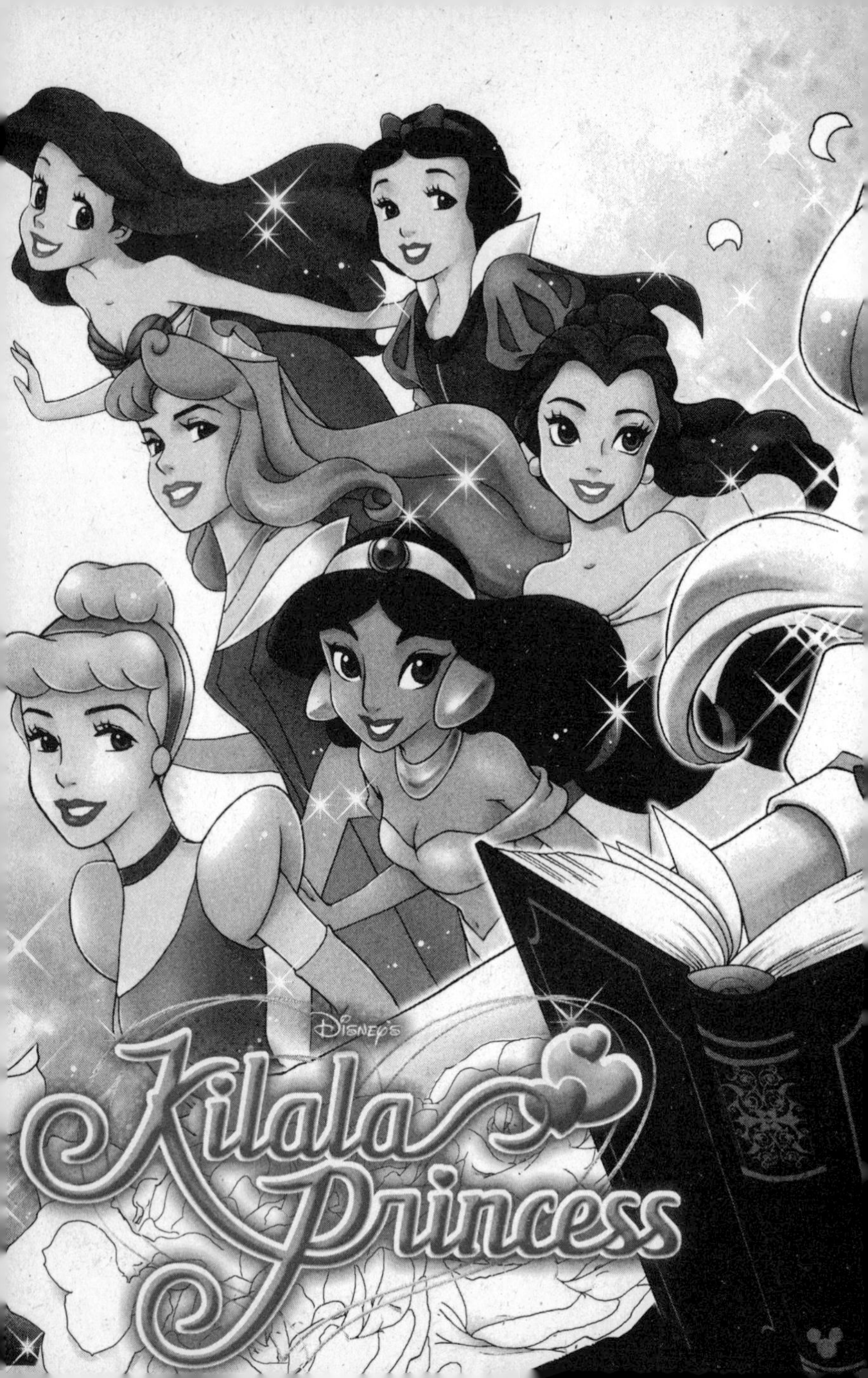
Disney's
Kilala Princess

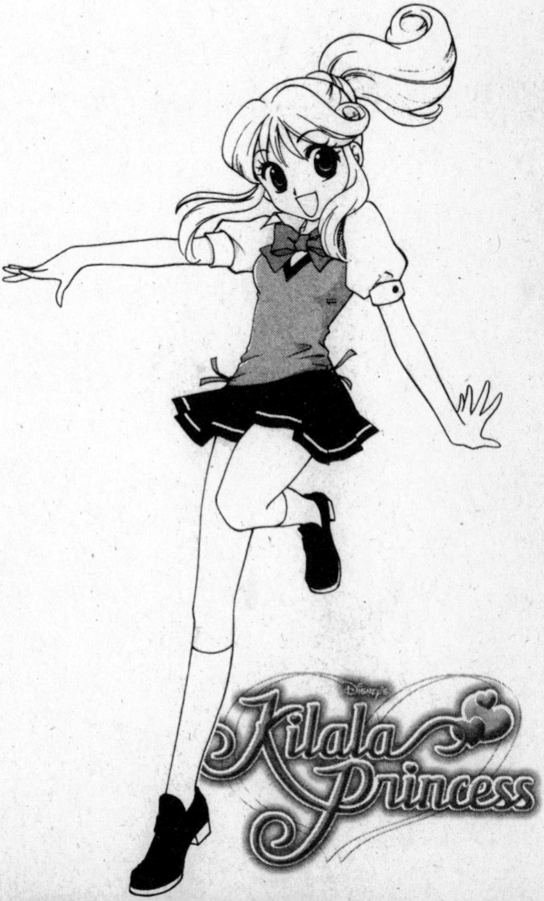
Disney's
Kilala Princess

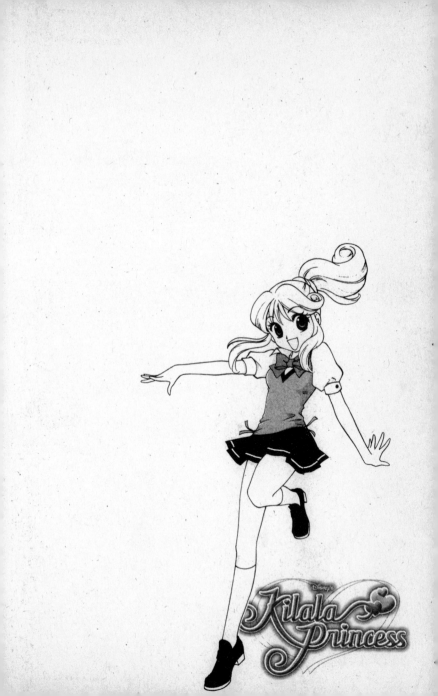

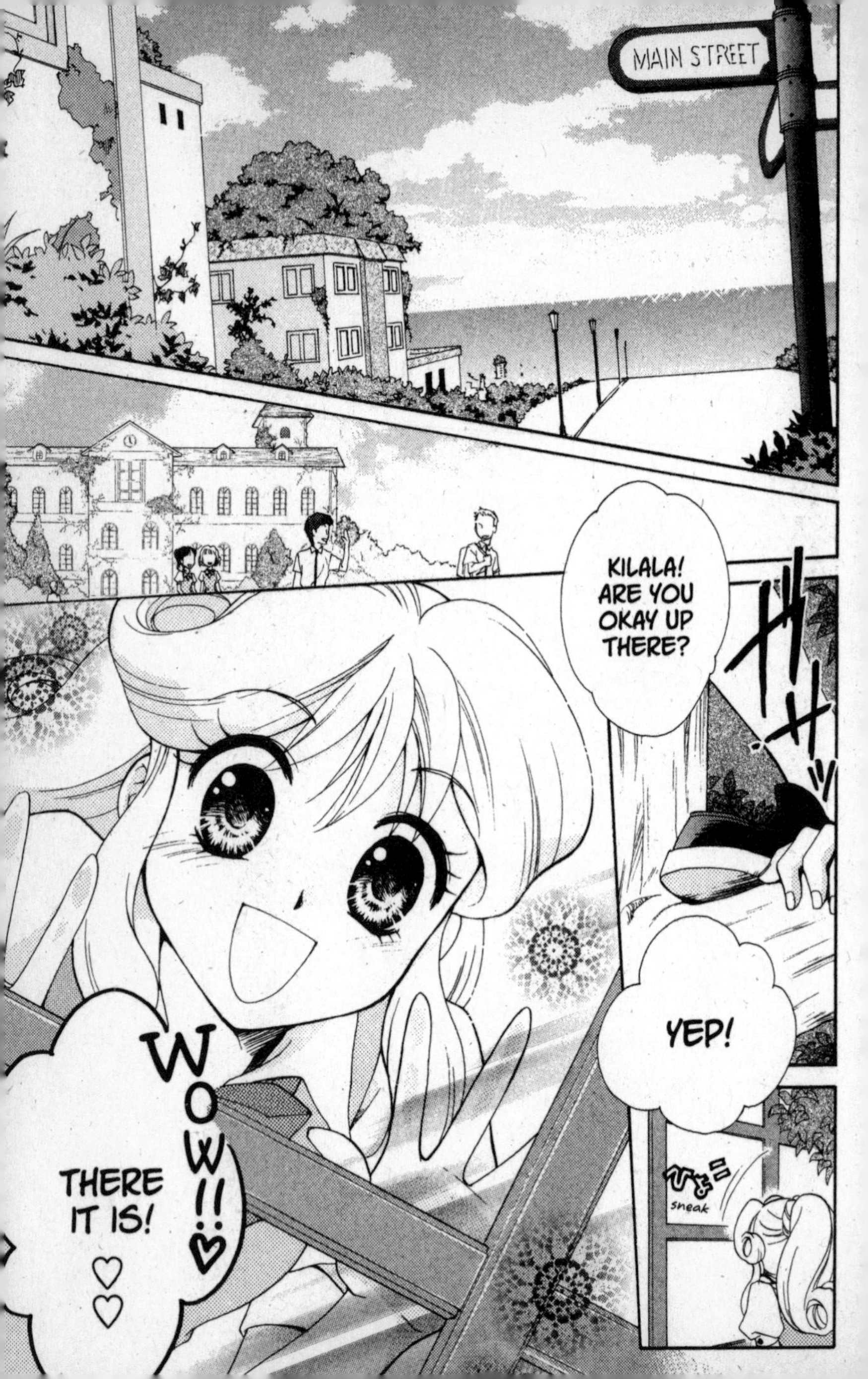
MAIN STREET
KILALA! ARE YOU OKAY UP THERE?
YEP!
sneak
WOW!! ♥
THERE IT IS! ♡ ♡

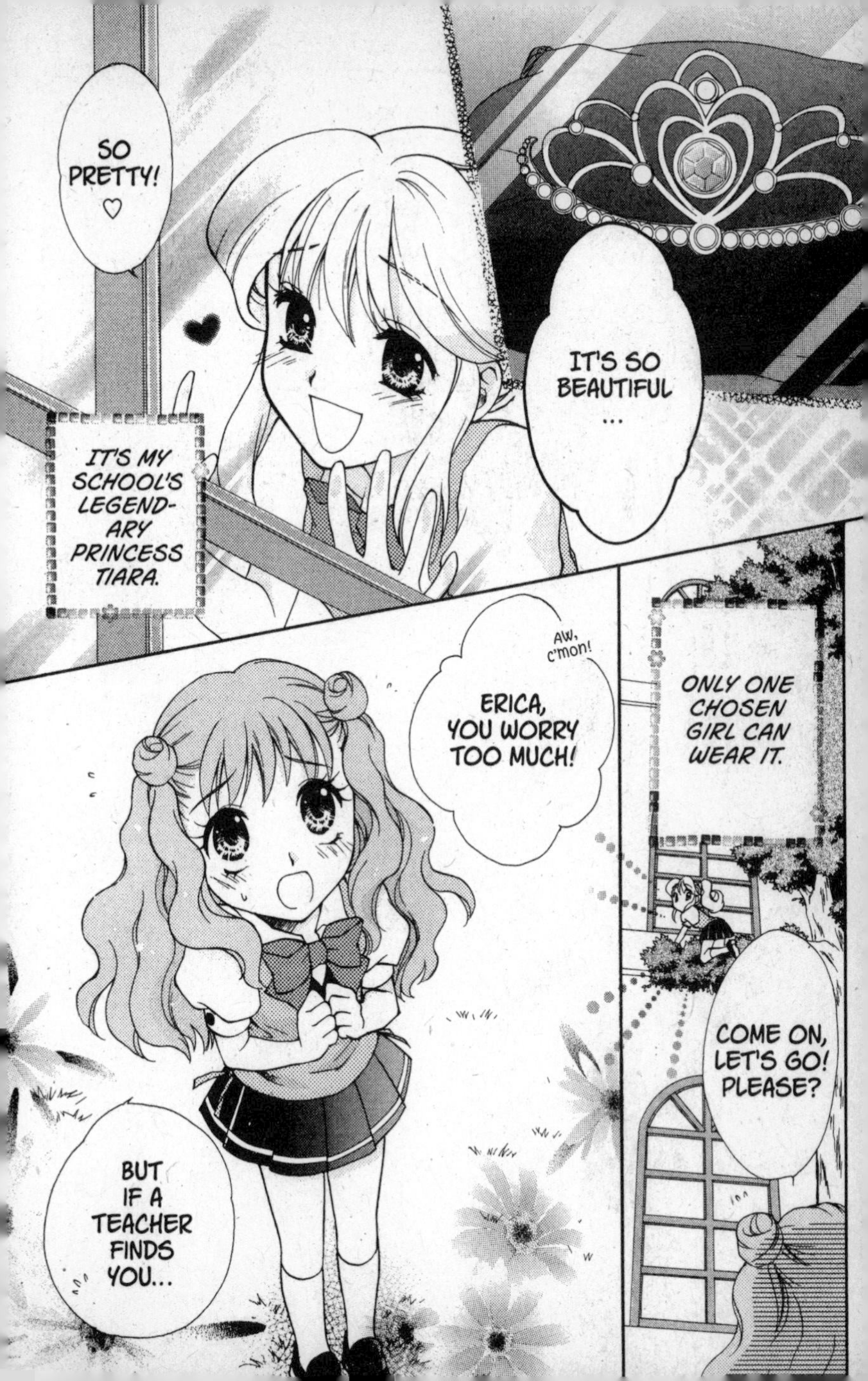
IT'S SO BEAUTIFUL ...
SO PRETTY! ♡
IT'S MY SCHOOL'S LEGENDARY PRINCESS TIARA.
ONLY ONE CHOSEN GIRL CAN WEAR IT.
COME ON, LET'S GO! PLEASE?
AW, C'mon!
ERICA, YOU WORRY TOO MUCH!
BUT IF A TEACHER FINDS YOU...

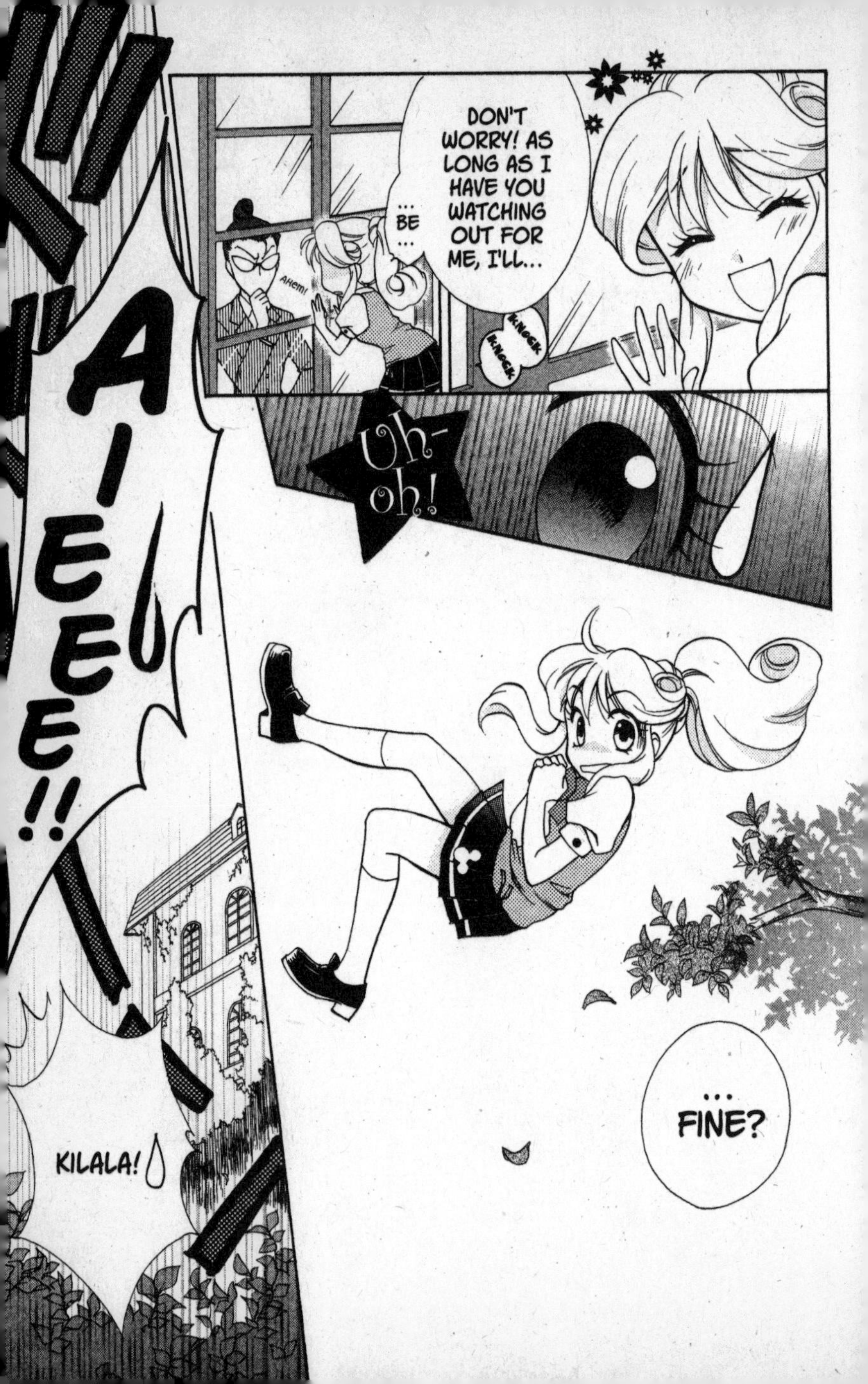
DON'T WORRY! AS LONG AS I HAVE YOU WATCHING OUT FOR ME, I'LL...
... BE ...
KNOCK KNOCK
AHEM!
Uh-oh!
... FINE?
AIEEEE!!
KILALA!

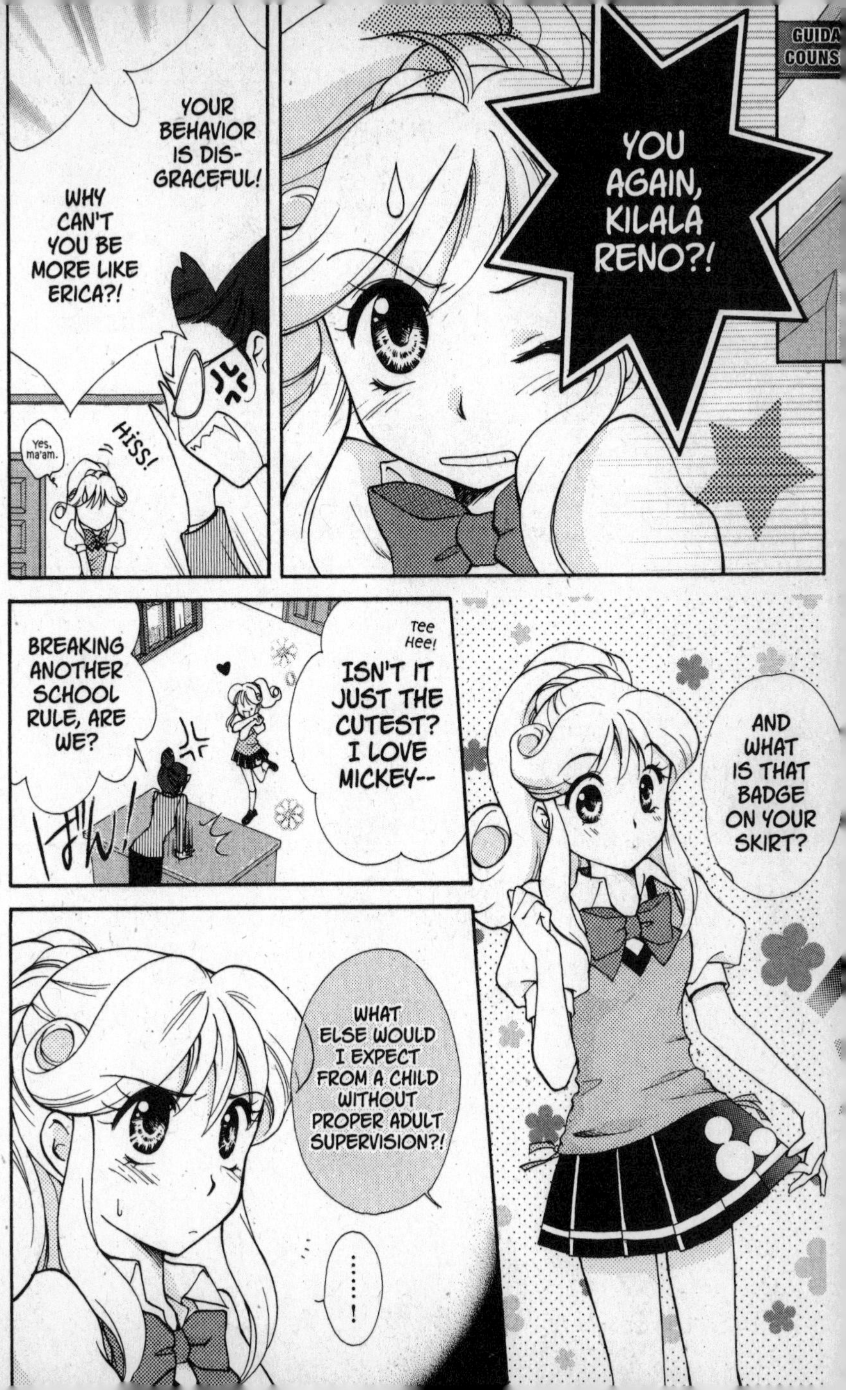
YOU AGAIN, KILALA RENO?!
YOUR BEHAVIOR IS DIS-GRACEFUL!
WHY CAN'T YOU BE MORE LIKE ERICA?!
HISS!
Yes, ma'am.
AND WHAT IS THAT BADGE ON YOUR SKIRT?
Tee Hee!
ISN'T IT JUST THE CUTEST? I LOVE MICKEY--
BREAKING ANOTHER SCHOOL RULE, ARE WE?
WHAT ELSE WOULD I EXPECT FROM A CHILD WITHOUT PROPER ADULT SUPERVISION?!
......!

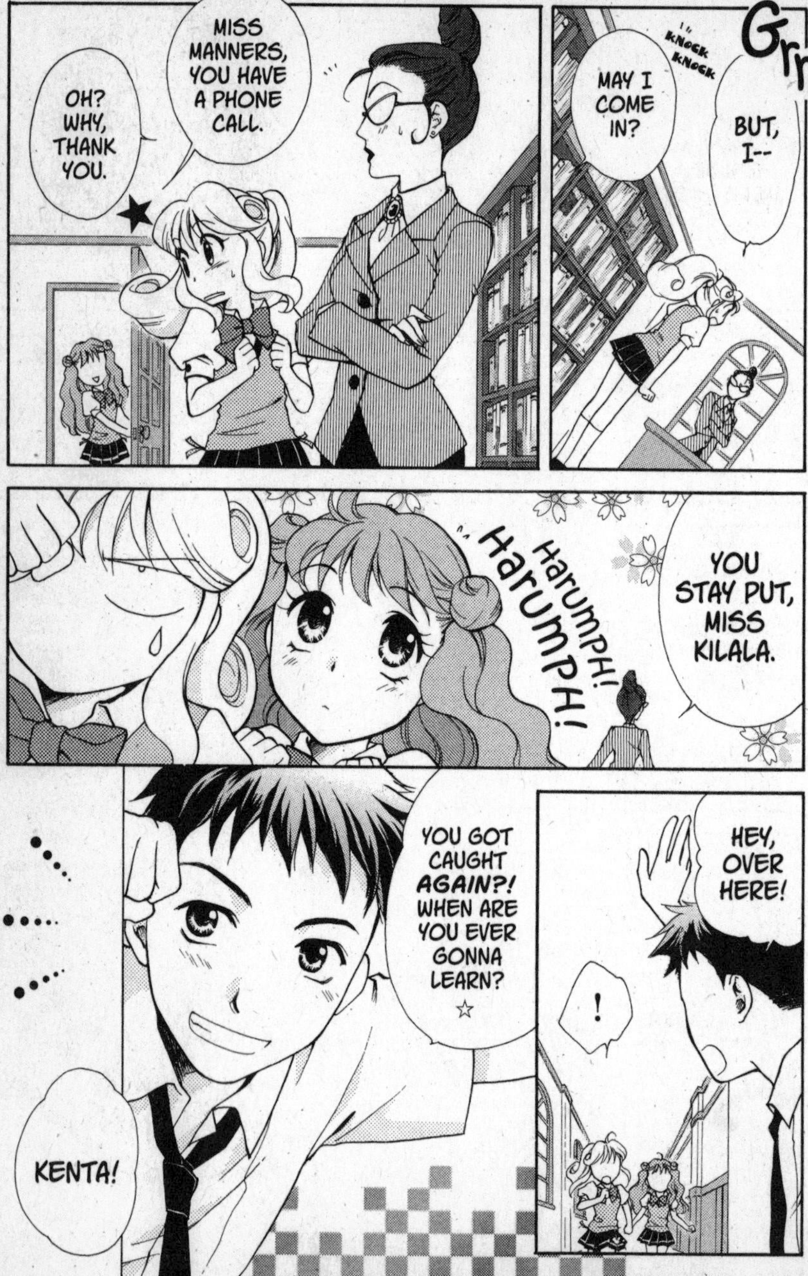
Grr!
BUT, I--
KNOCK KNOCK
MAY I COME IN?
MISS MANNERS, YOU HAVE A PHONE CALL.
OH? WHY, THANK YOU.
YOU STAY PUT, MISS KILALA.
HARUMPH! HARUMPH!
HEY, OVER HERE!
!
YOU GOT CAUGHT **AGAIN?!** WHEN ARE YOU EVER GONNA LEARN? ☆
...
....
....
KENTA!

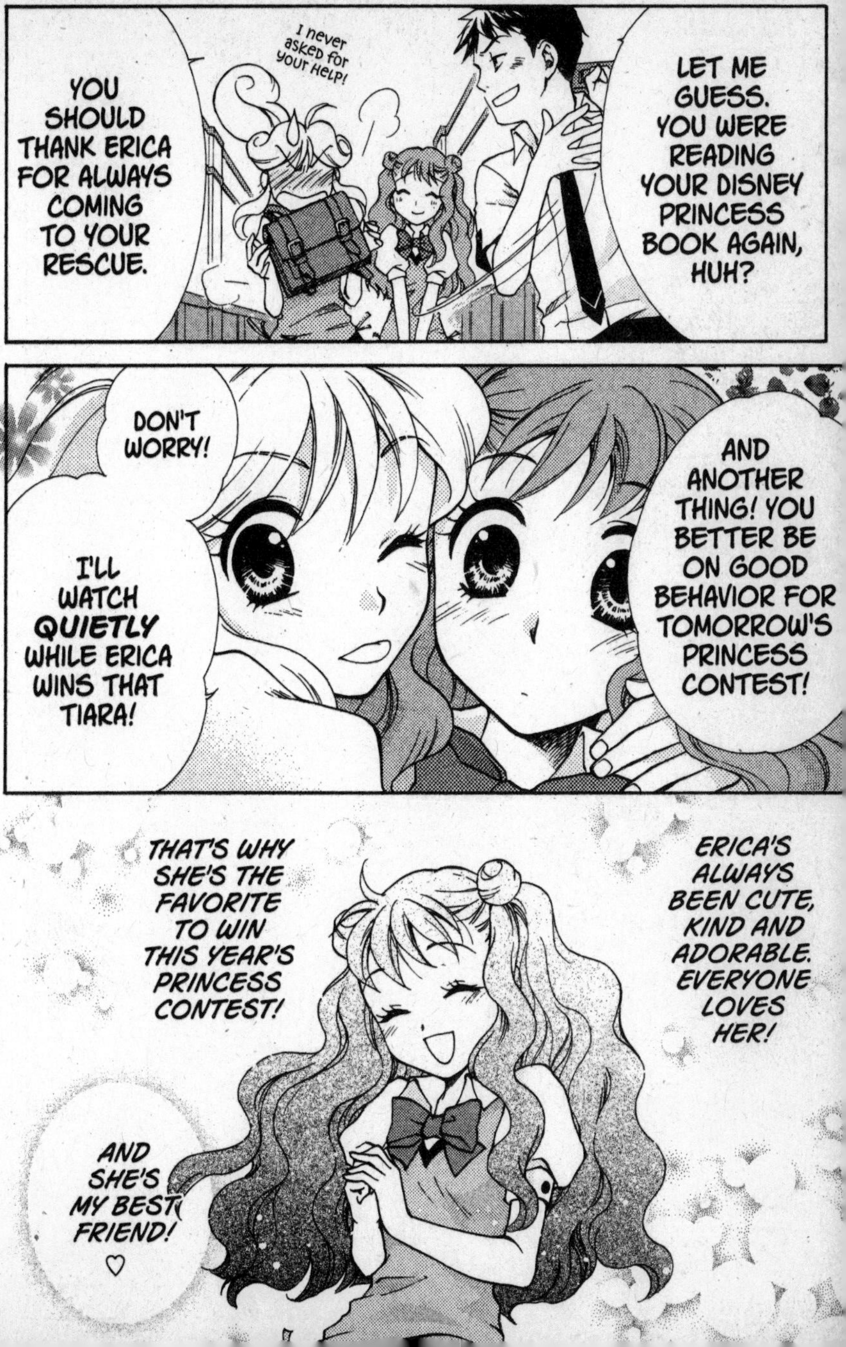
LET ME GUESS. YOU WERE READING YOUR DISNEY PRINCESS BOOK AGAIN, HUH?
I never asked for your Help!
YOU SHOULD THANK ERICA FOR ALWAYS COMING TO YOUR RESCUE.
AND ANOTHER THING! YOU BETTER BE ON GOOD BEHAVIOR FOR TOMORROW'S PRINCESS CONTEST!
DON'T WORRY!
I'LL WATCH QUIETLY WHILE ERICA WINS THAT TIARA!
ERICA'S ALWAYS BEEN CUTE, KIND AND ADORABLE. EVERYONE LOVES HER!
THAT'S WHY SHE'S THE FAVORITE TO WIN THIS YEAR'S PRINCESS CONTEST!
AND SHE'S MY BEST FRIEND! ♡

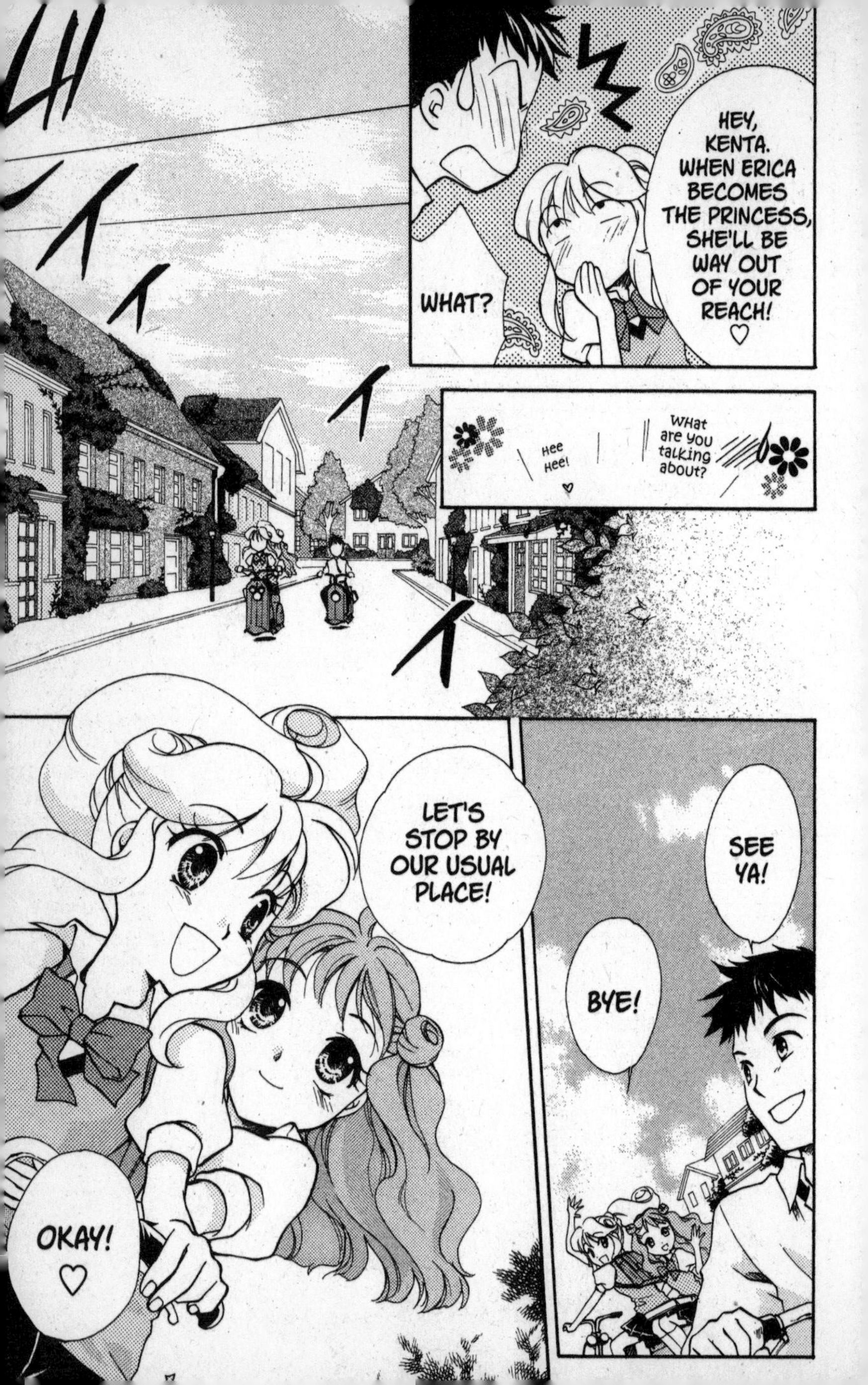
HEY, KENTA. WHEN ERICA BECOMES THE PRINCESS, SHE'LL BE WAY OUT OF YOUR REACH! ♡
WHAT?
What are you talking about?
Hee Hee! ♡
SEE YA!
BYE!
LET'S STOP BY OUR USUAL PLACE!
OKAY! ♡

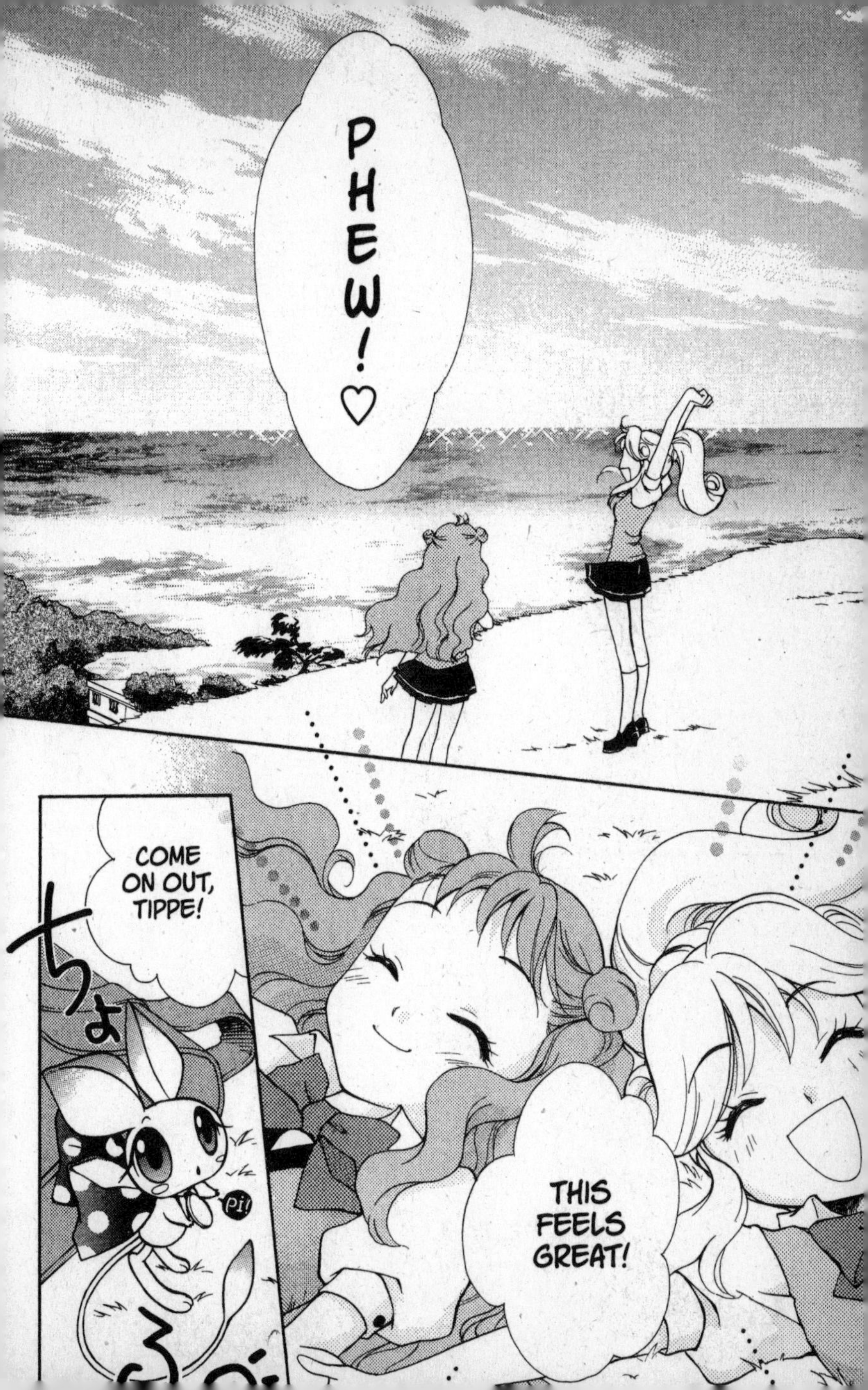
PHEW! ♡
THIS FEELS GREAT!
COME ON OUT, TIPPE!
ちょ
PI!

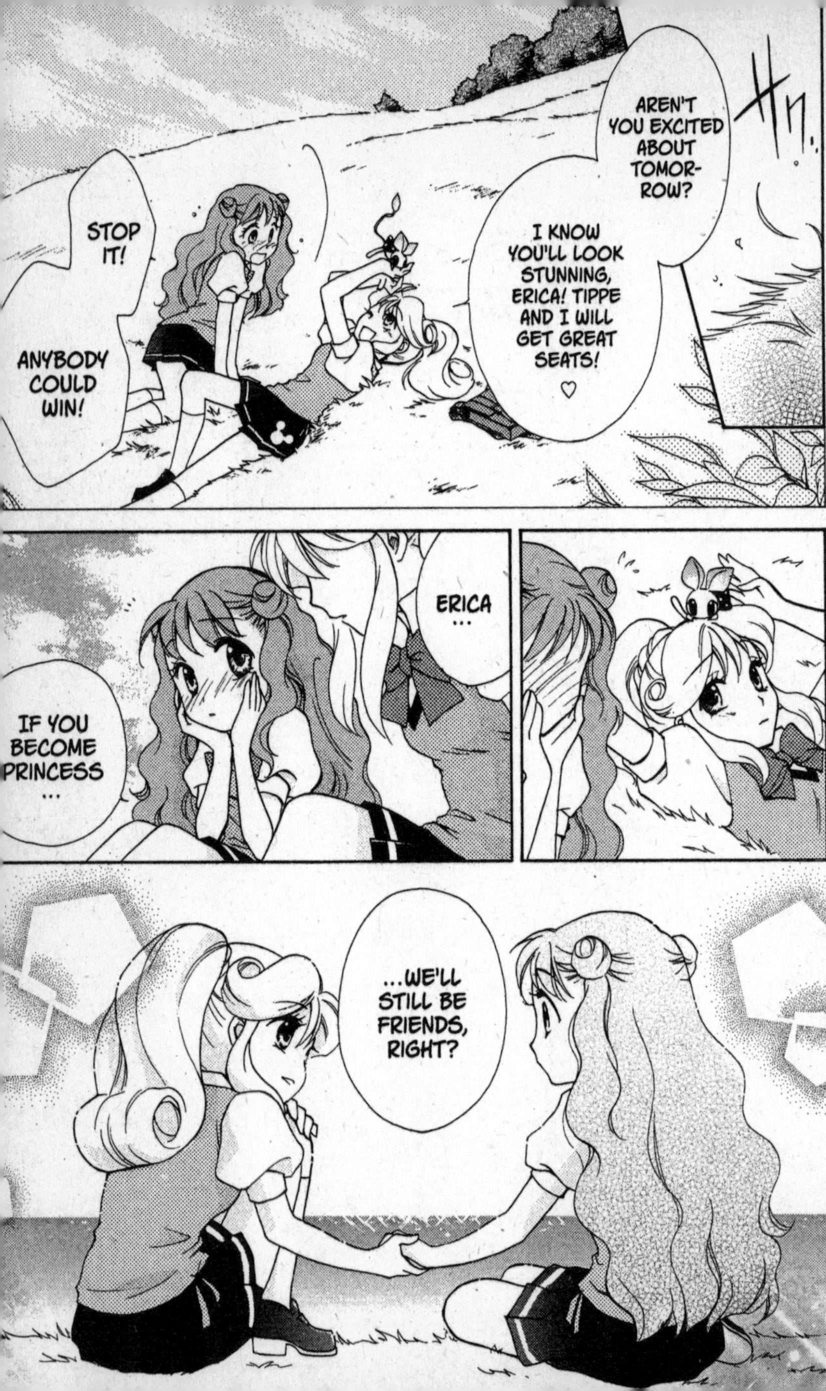
AREN'T YOU EXCITED ABOUT TOMOR-ROW?
I KNOW YOU'LL LOOK STUNNING, ERICA! TIPPE AND I WILL GET GREAT SEATS! ♡
STOP IT!
ANYBODY COULD WIN!
ERICA ...
IF YOU BECOME PRINCESS ...
...WE'LL STILL BE FRIENDS, RIGHT?

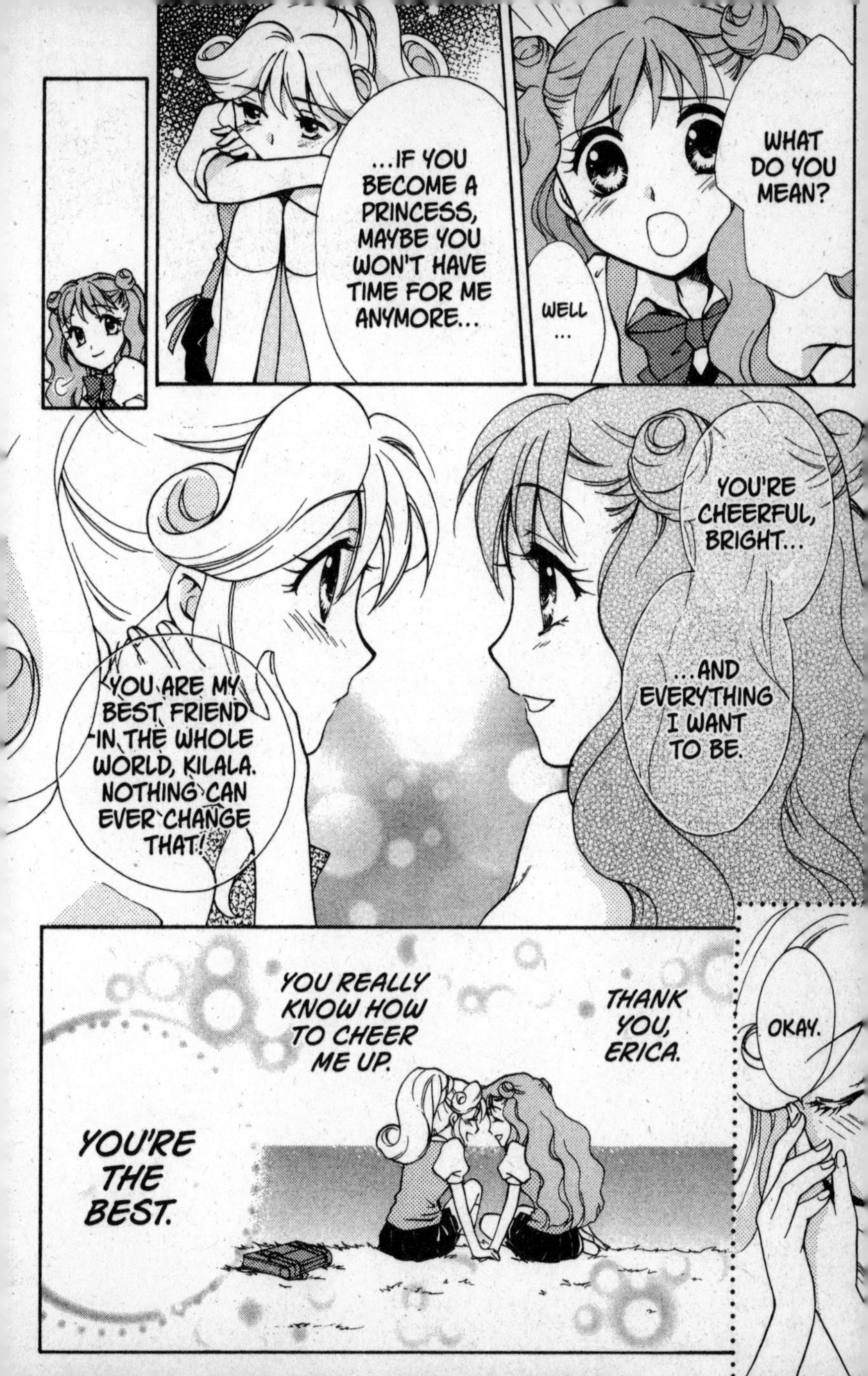
WHAT DO YOU MEAN?
WELL ...
...IF YOU BECOME A PRINCESS, MAYBE YOU WON'T HAVE TIME FOR ME ANYMORE...
YOU'RE CHEERFUL, BRIGHT...
...AND EVERYTHING I WANT TO BE.
YOU ARE MY BEST FRIEND IN THE WHOLE WORLD, KILALA. NOTHING CAN EVER CHANGE THAT!
OKAY.
THANK YOU, ERICA.
YOU REALLY KNOW HOW TO CHEER ME UP.
YOU'RE THE BEST.

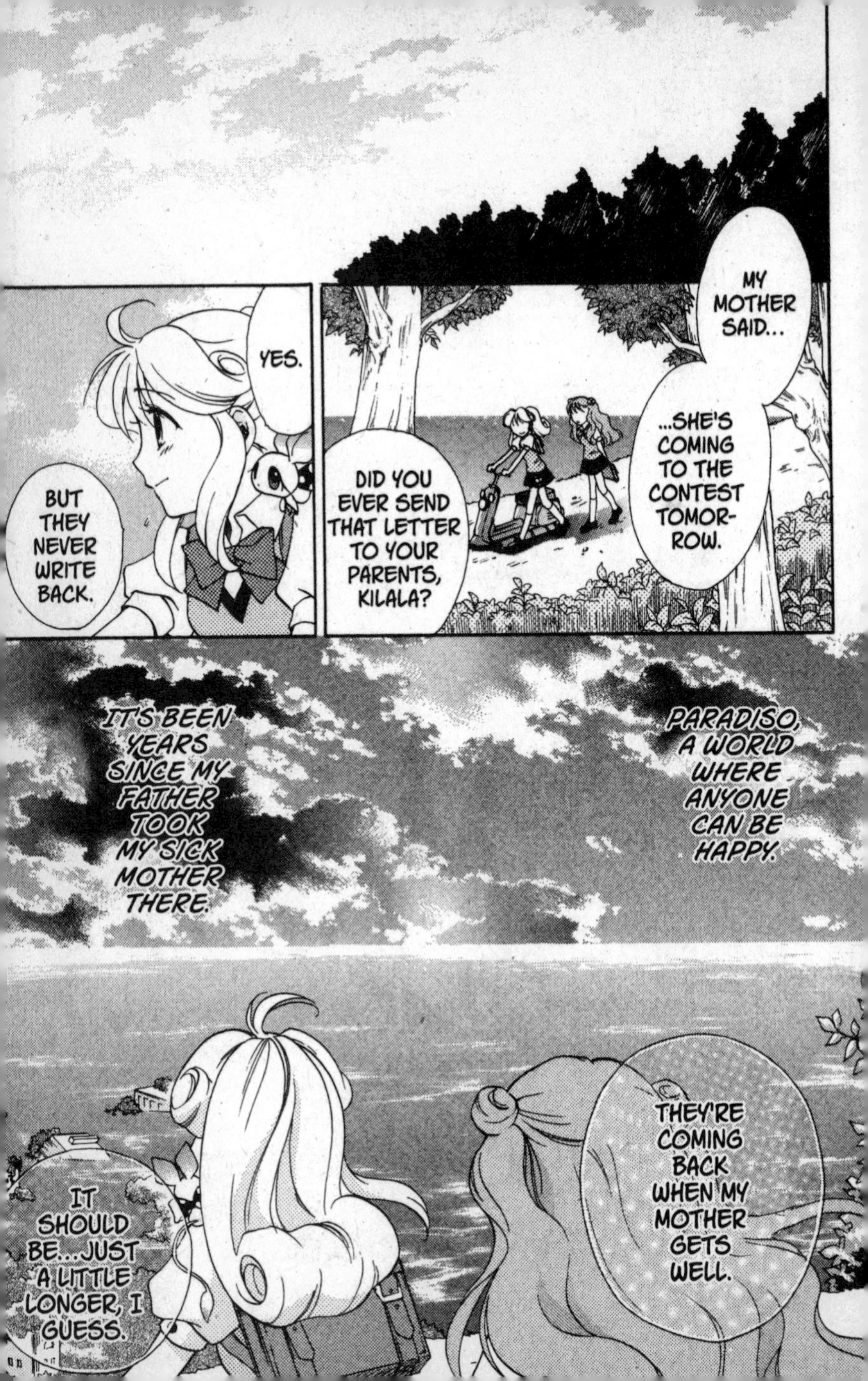
MY MOTHER SAID...
...SHE'S COMING TO THE CONTEST TOMOR-ROW.
DID YOU EVER SEND THAT LETTER TO YOUR PARENTS, KILALA?
YES.
BUT THEY NEVER WRITE BACK.
PARADISO, A WORLD WHERE ANYONE CAN BE HAPPY.
IT'S BEEN YEARS SINCE MY FATHER TOOK MY SICK MOTHER THERE.
THEY'RE COMING BACK WHEN MY MOTHER GETS WELL.
IT SHOULD BE...JUST A LITTLE LONGER, I GUESS.

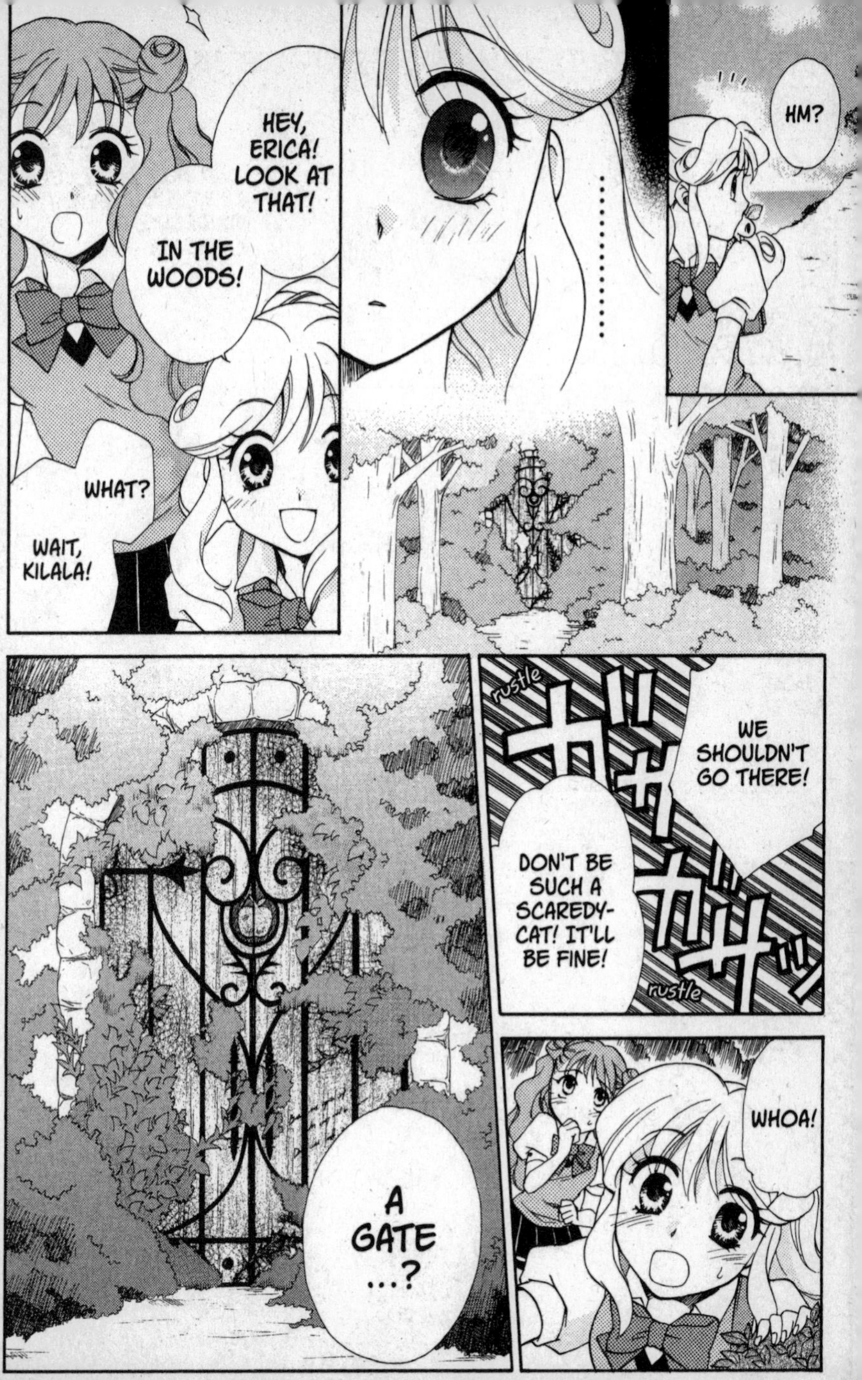
HM?
HEY, ERICA! LOOK AT THAT!
IN THE WOODS!
WHAT?
WAIT, KILALA!
rustle
ガサ
ガサッ
rustle
WE SHOULDN'T GO THERE!
DON'T BE SUCH A SCAREDY-CAT! IT'LL BE FINE!
WHOA!
A GATE ...?

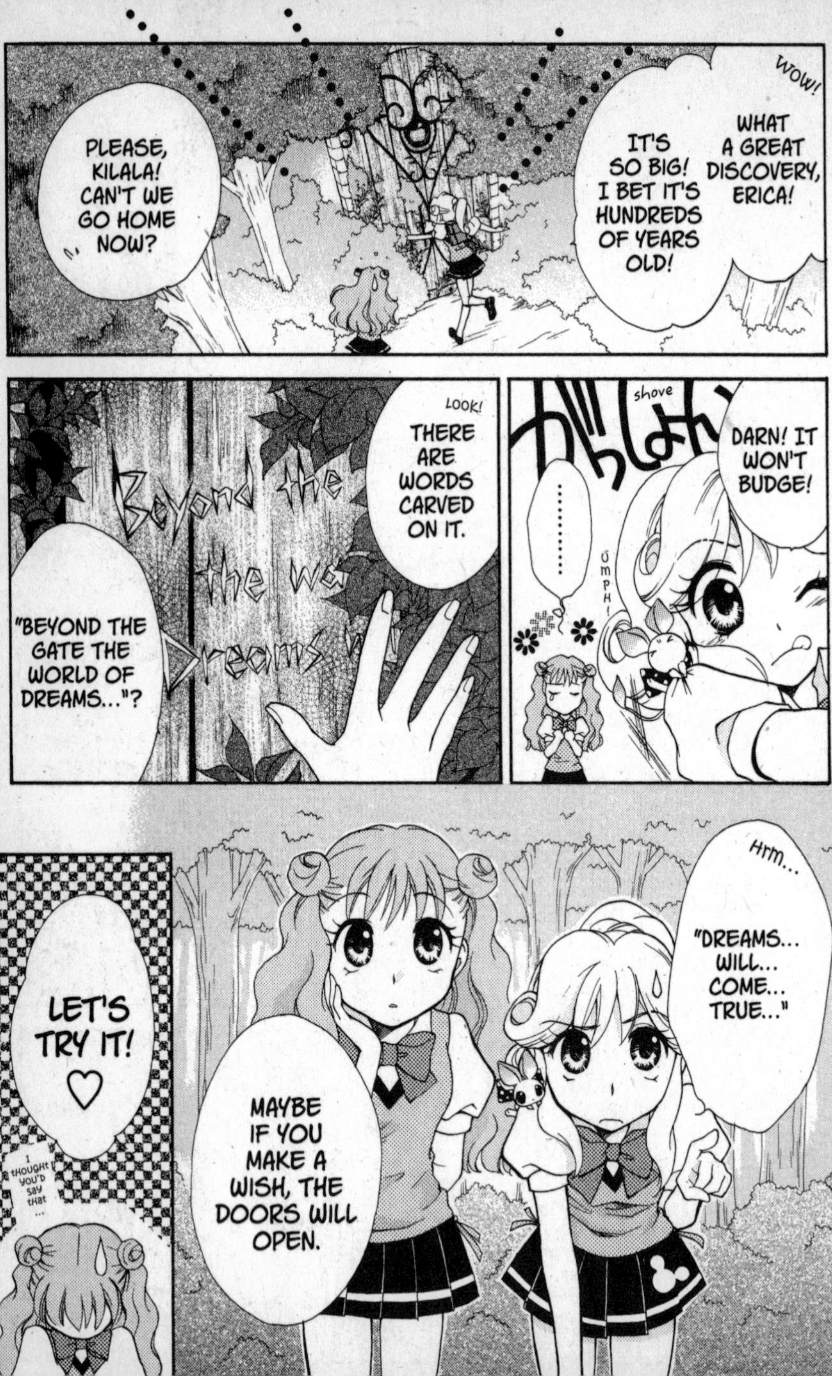
WOW!
WHAT A GREAT DISCOVERY, ERICA!
IT'S SO BIG! I BET IT'S HUNDREDS OF YEARS OLD!
PLEASE, KILALA! CAN'T WE GO HOME NOW?
shove
DARN! IT WON'T BUDGE!
UMPH!
......
LOOK!
THERE ARE WORDS CARVED ON IT.
Beyond the
the wa
Dreams w
"BEYOND THE GATE THE WORLD OF DREAMS..."?
Hrm...
"DREAMS... WILL... COME... TRUE..."
MAYBE IF YOU MAKE A WISH, THE DOORS WILL OPEN.
LET'S TRY IT! ♡
I thought you'd say that ...

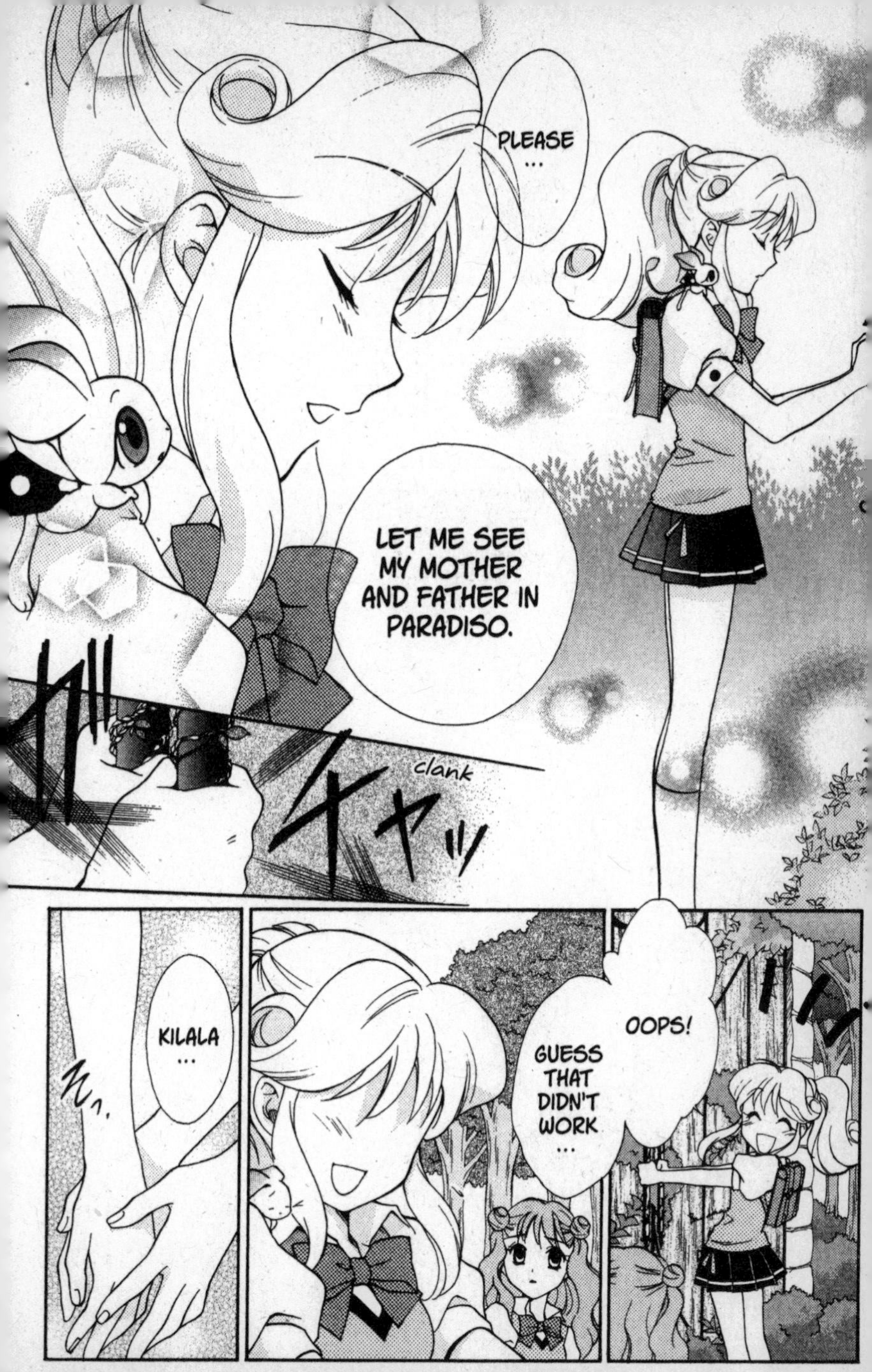
PLEASE ...
LET ME SEE MY MOTHER AND FATHER IN PARADISO.
clank
OOPS!
GUESS THAT DIDN'T WORK ...
KILALA ...

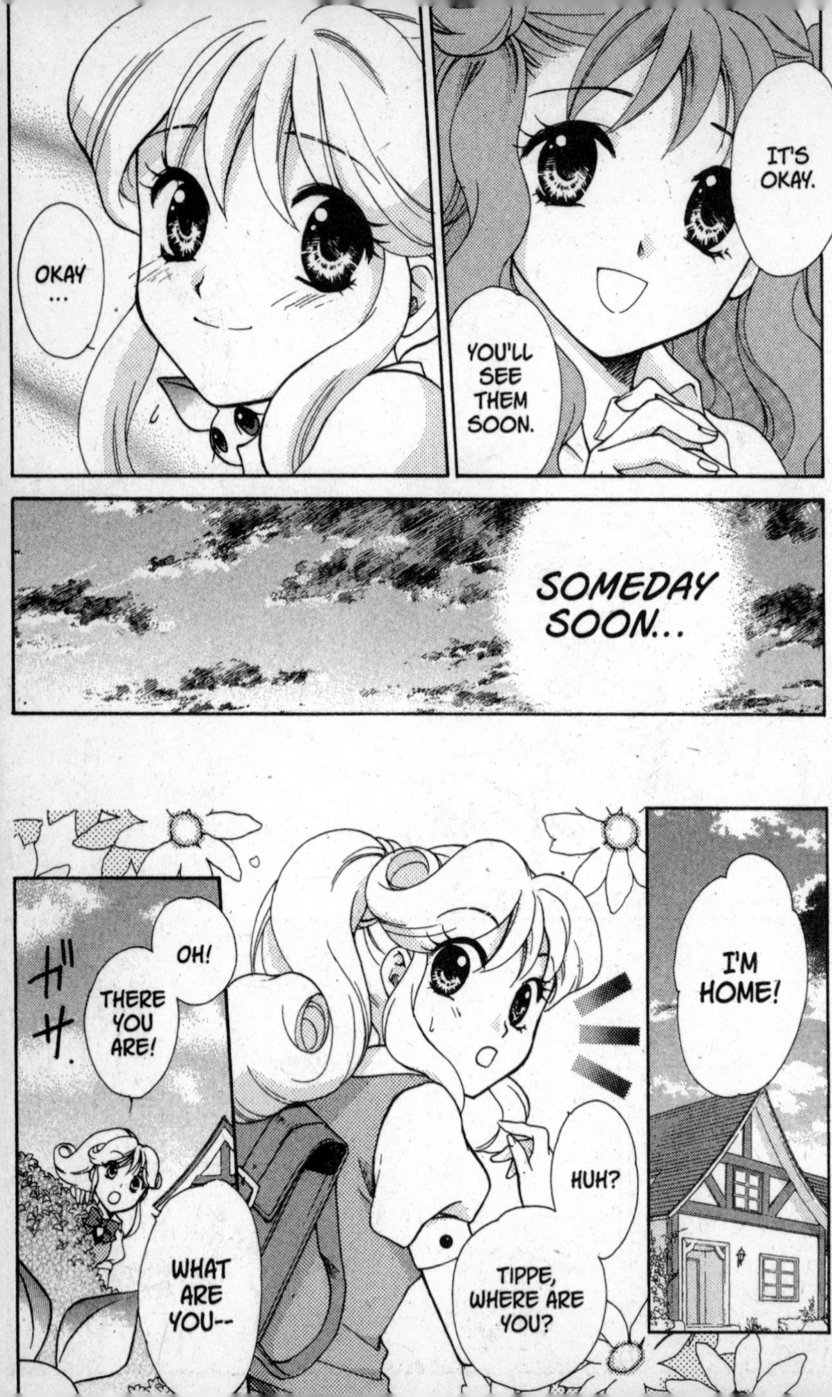
IT'S OKAY.
YOU'LL SEE THEM SOON.
OKAY ...
SOMEDAY SOON...
I'M HOME!
HUH?
TIPPE, WHERE ARE YOU?
ガサ
OH!
THERE YOU ARE!
WHAT ARE YOU--

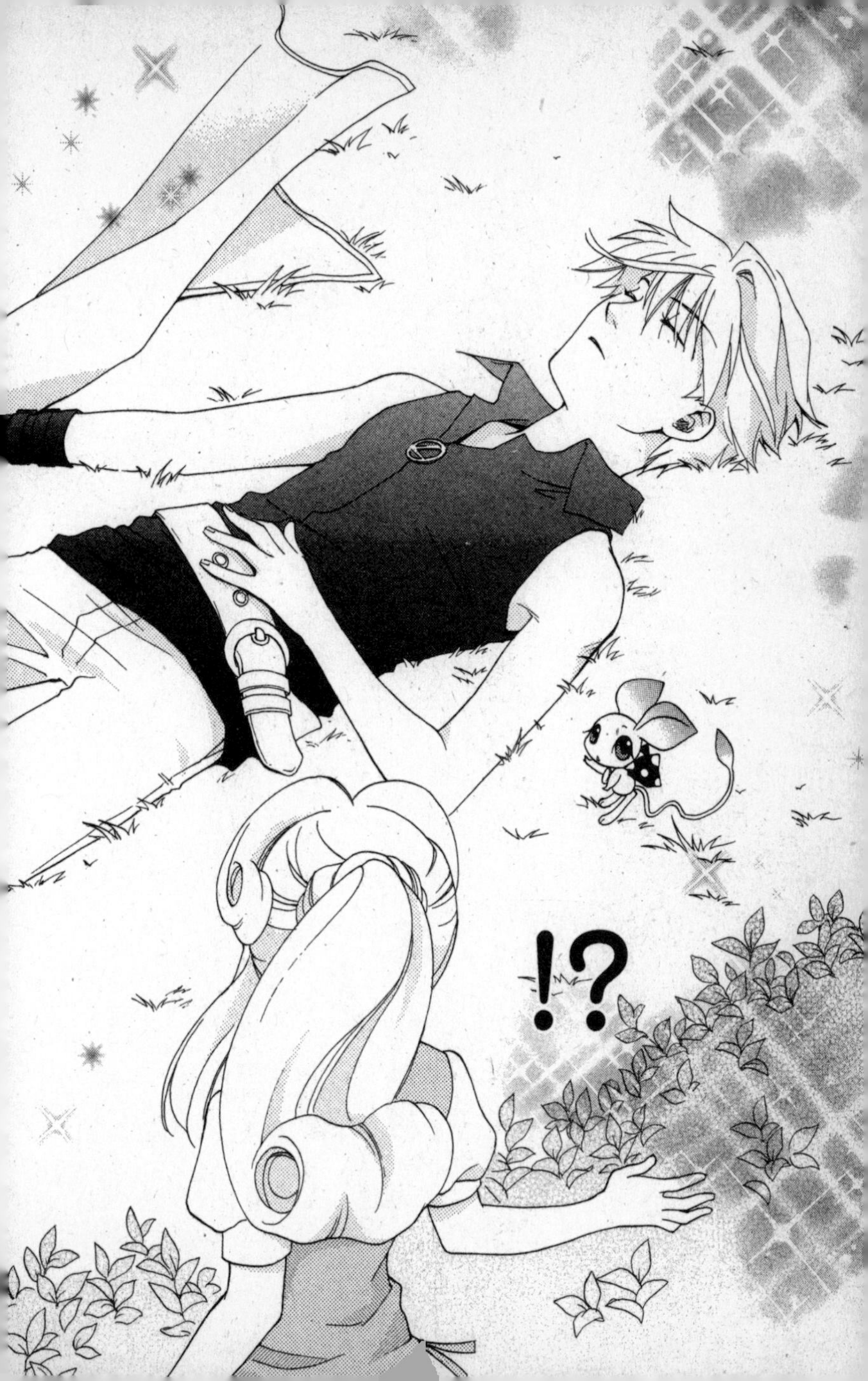
!?

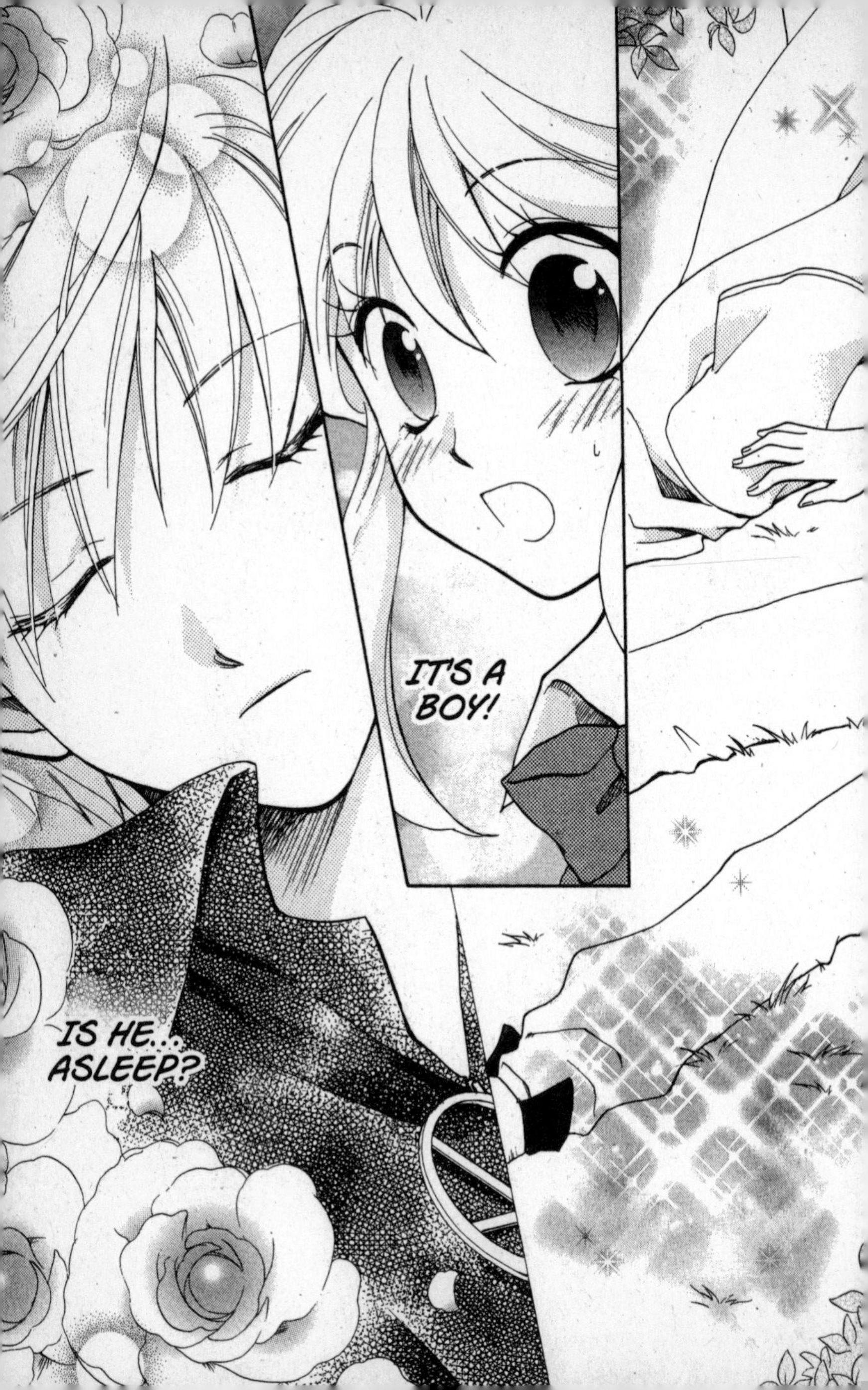
IT'S A BOY!
IS HE... ASLEEP?

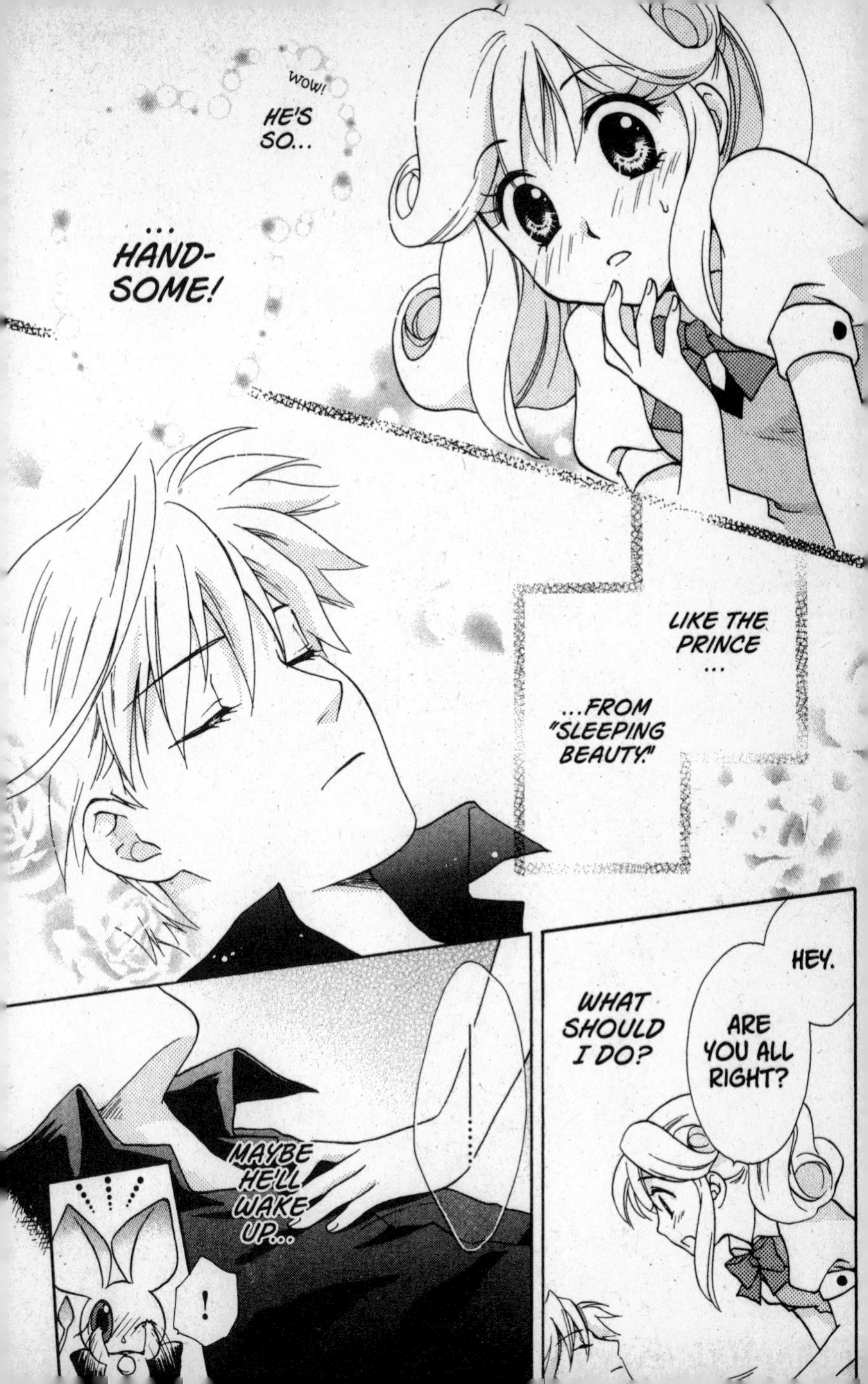
WOW!
HE'S SO...
...HAND-SOME!
LIKE THE PRINCE ...
...FROM "SLEEPING BEAUTY."
HEY.
ARE YOU ALL RIGHT?
WHAT SHOULD I DO?
MAYBE HE'LL WAKE UP...
!

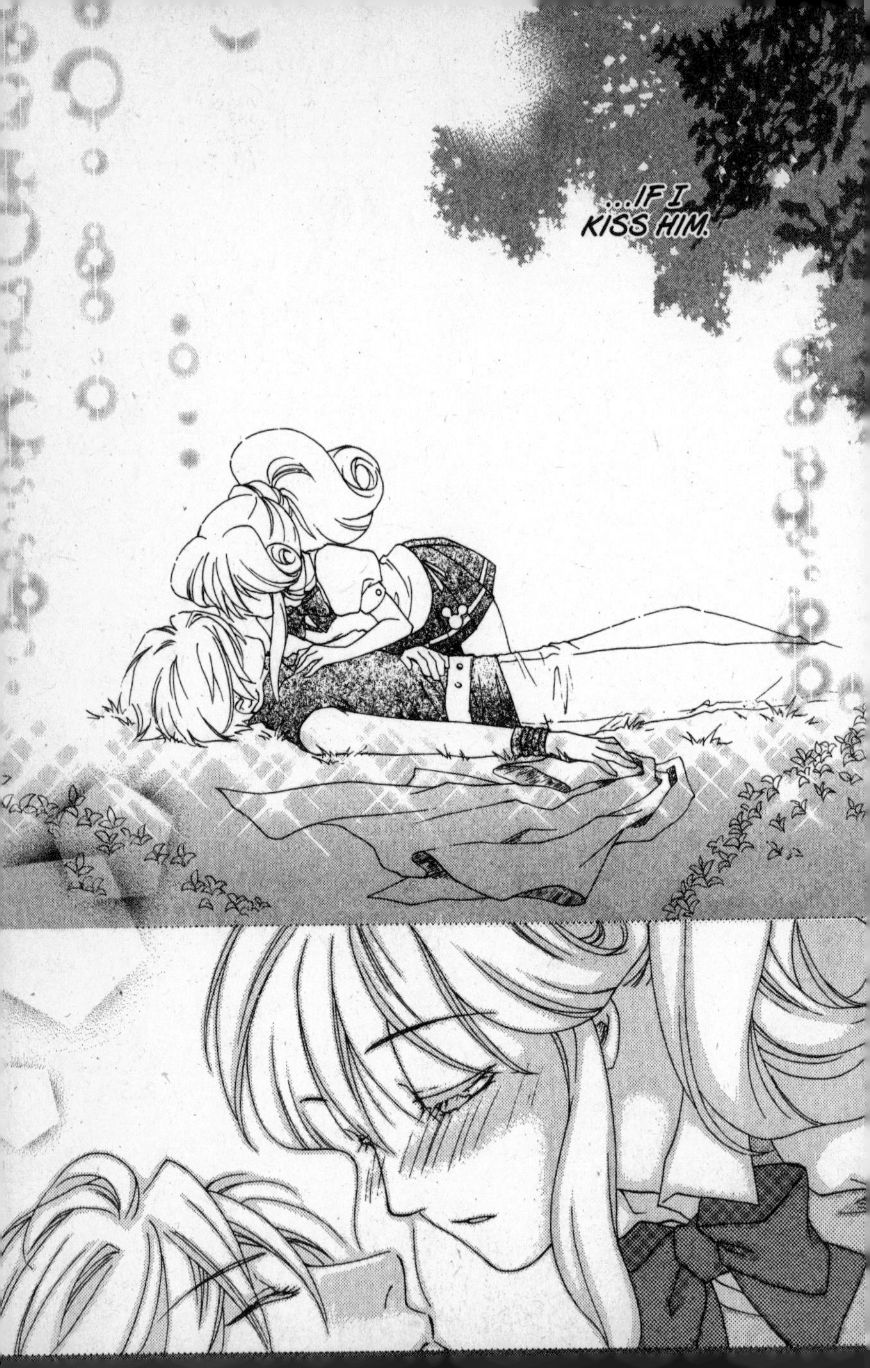
...IF I
KISS HIM.

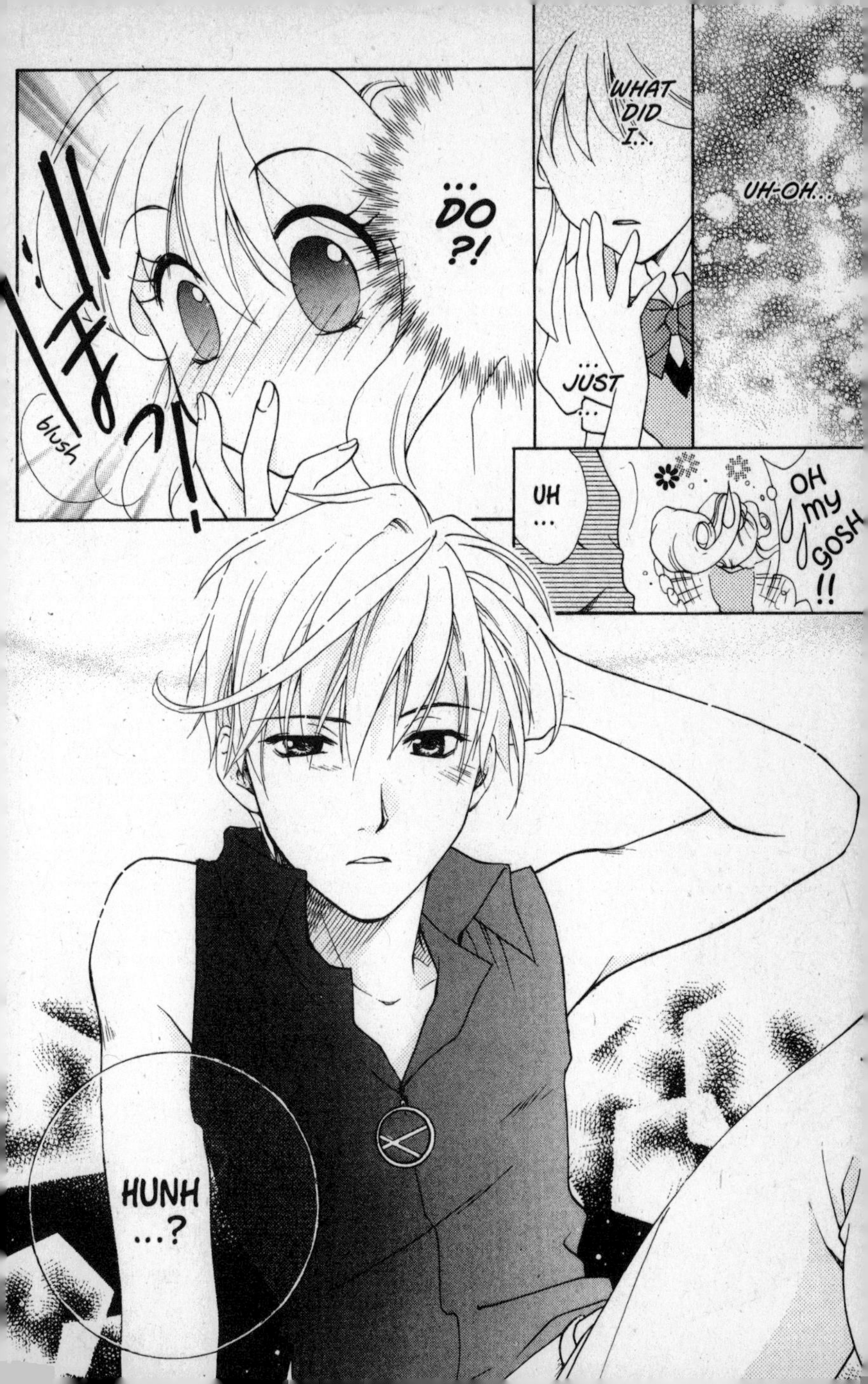
UH-OH...
WHAT DID I...
...JUST...
...DO?!
blush
OH my GOSH!!
UH...
HUNH...?

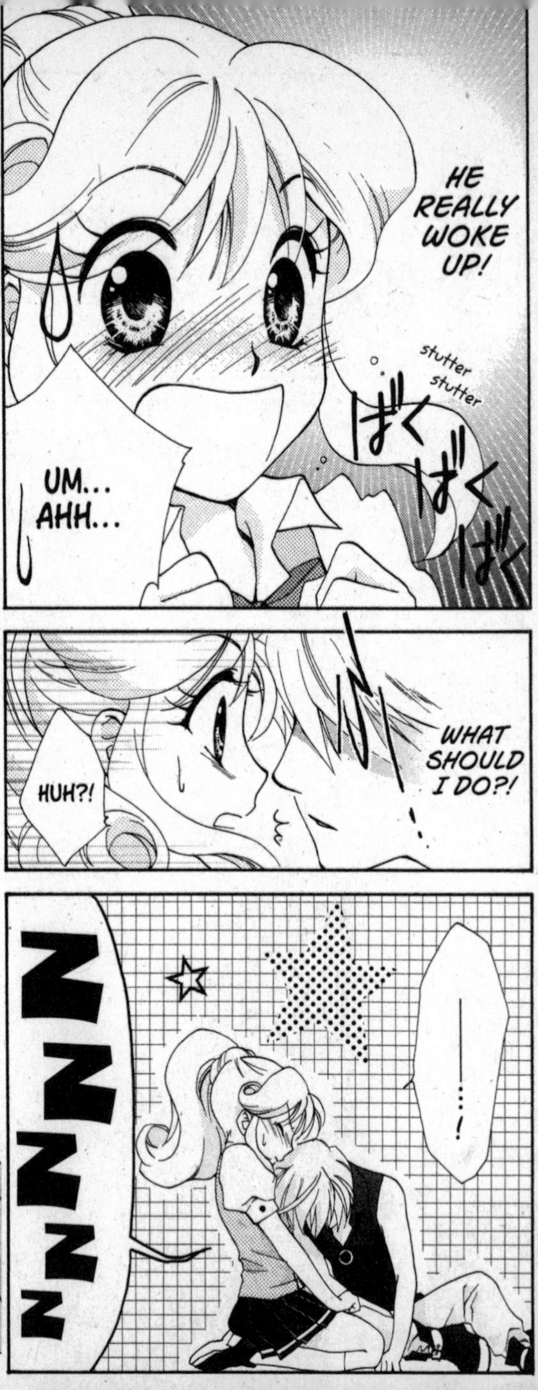
HE REALLY WOKE UP!
stutter stutter
ばくばくばく
UM... AHH...
WHAT SHOULD I DO?!
HUH?!
......!
ZZZZ

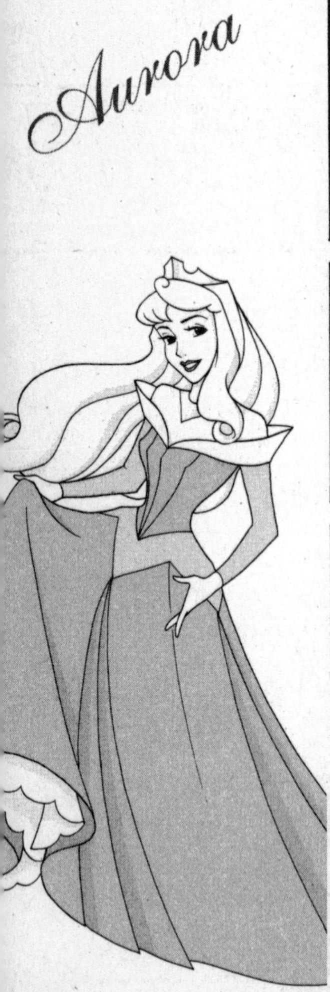
Aurora

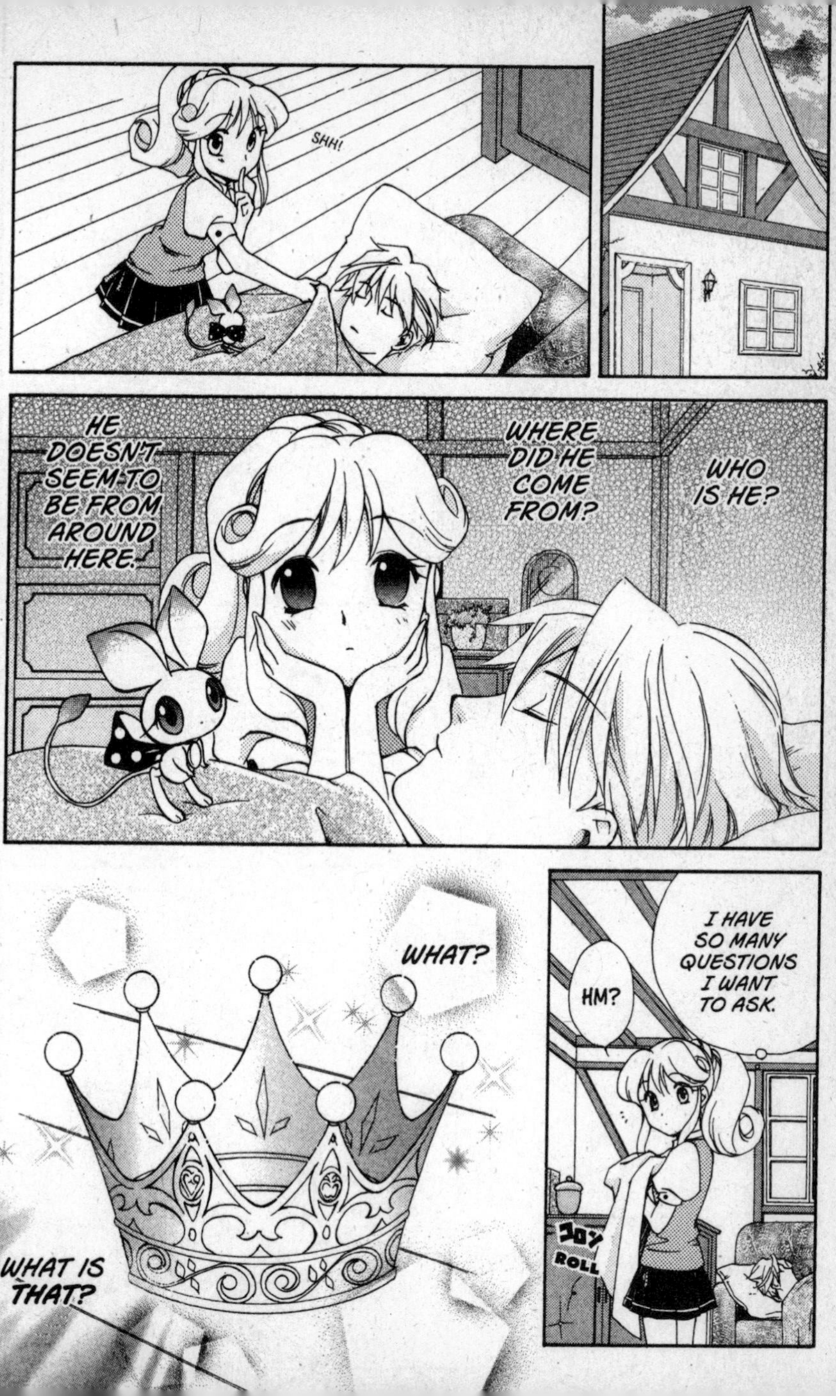
SHH!
WHO IS HE?
WHERE DID HE COME FROM?
HE DOESN'T SEEM TO BE FROM AROUND HERE.
I HAVE SO MANY QUESTIONS I WANT TO ASK.
HM?
コロッ
ROLL
WHAT?
WHAT IS THAT?

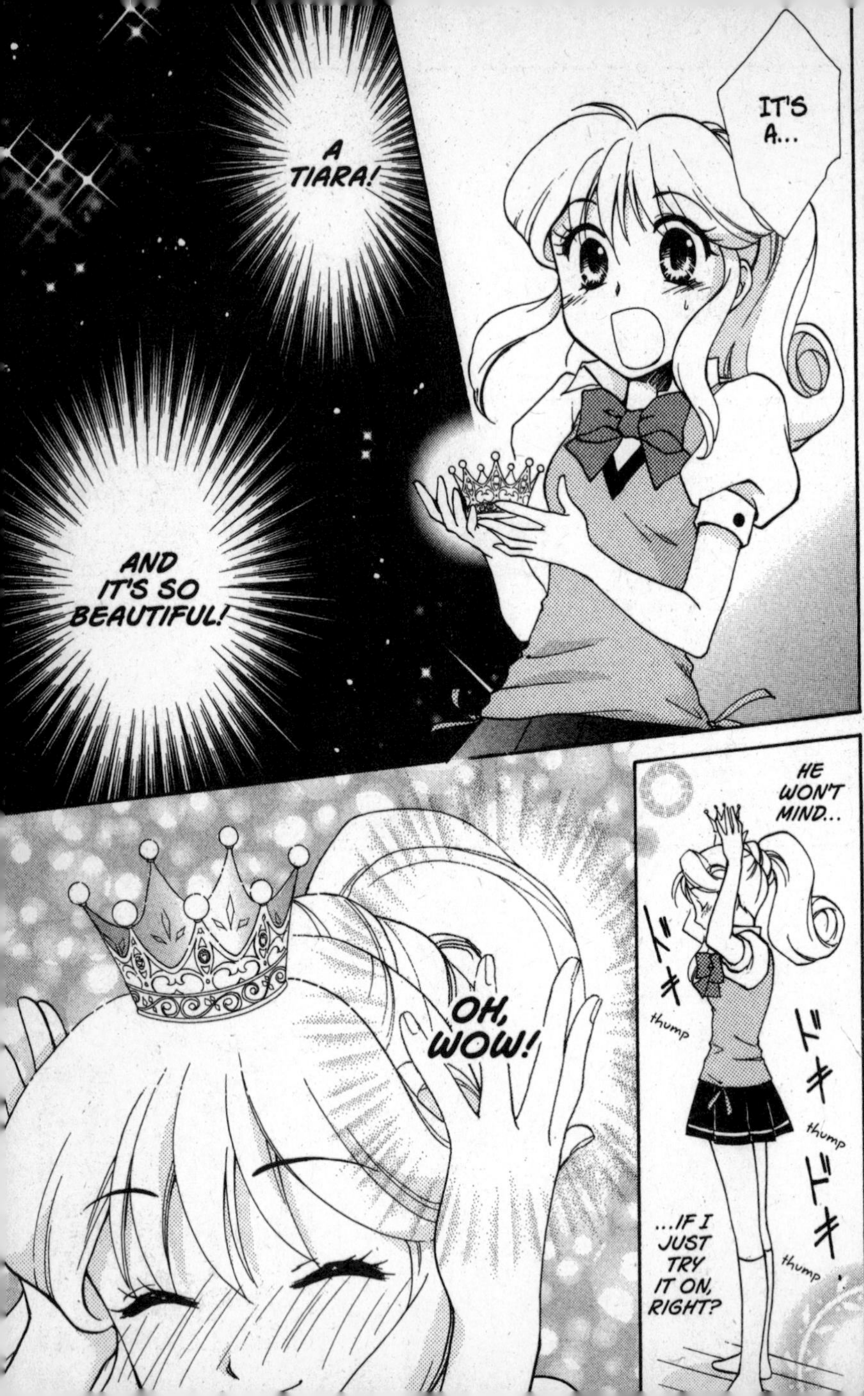
IT'S A...
A TIARA!
AND IT'S SO BEAUTIFUL!
HE WON'T MIND...
...IF I JUST TRY IT ON, RIGHT?
ドキ
thump
ドキ
thump
ドキ
thump
OH, WOW!

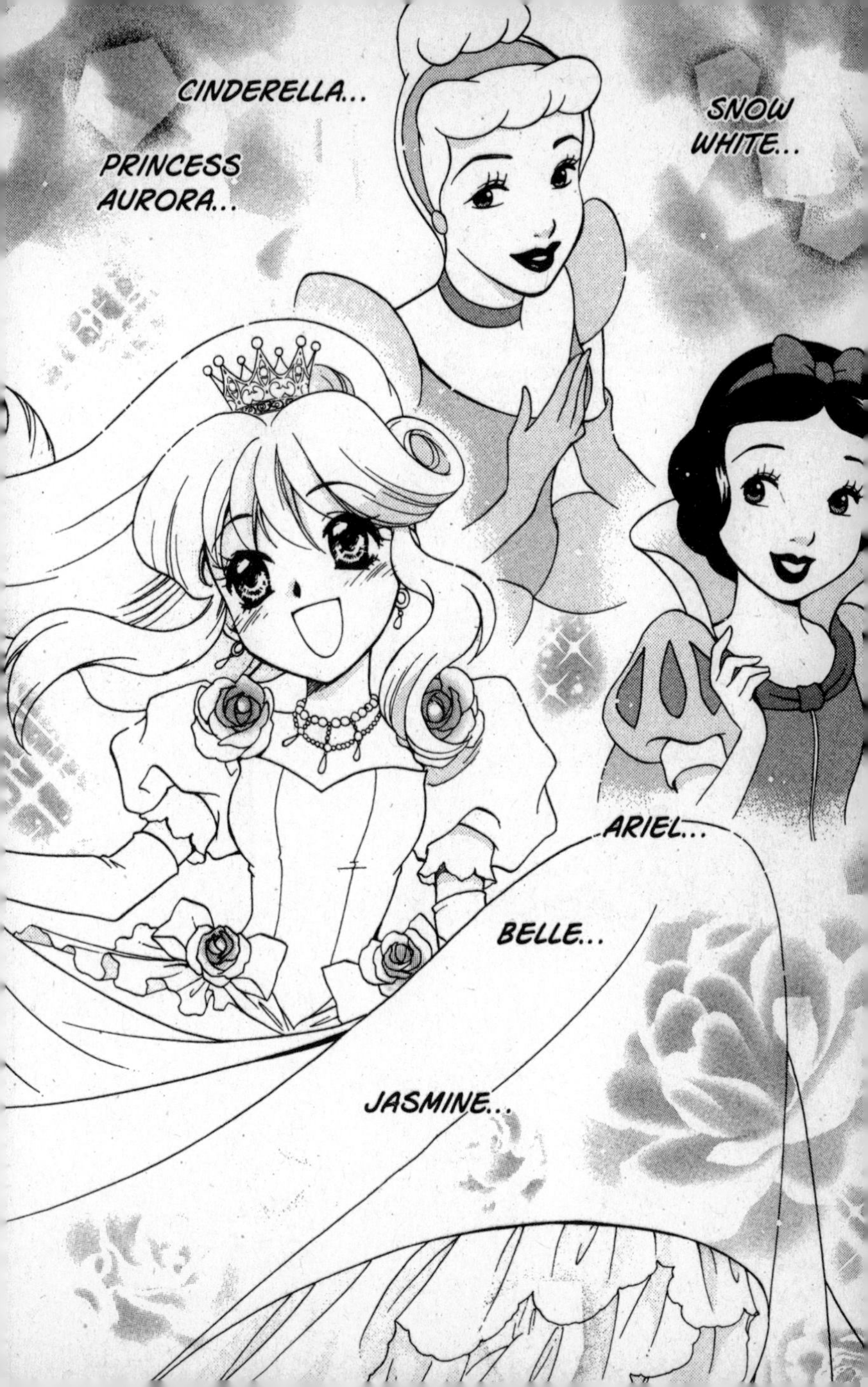
SNOW WHITE...
CINDERELLA...
PRINCESS AURORA...
ARIEL...
BELLE...
JASMINE...

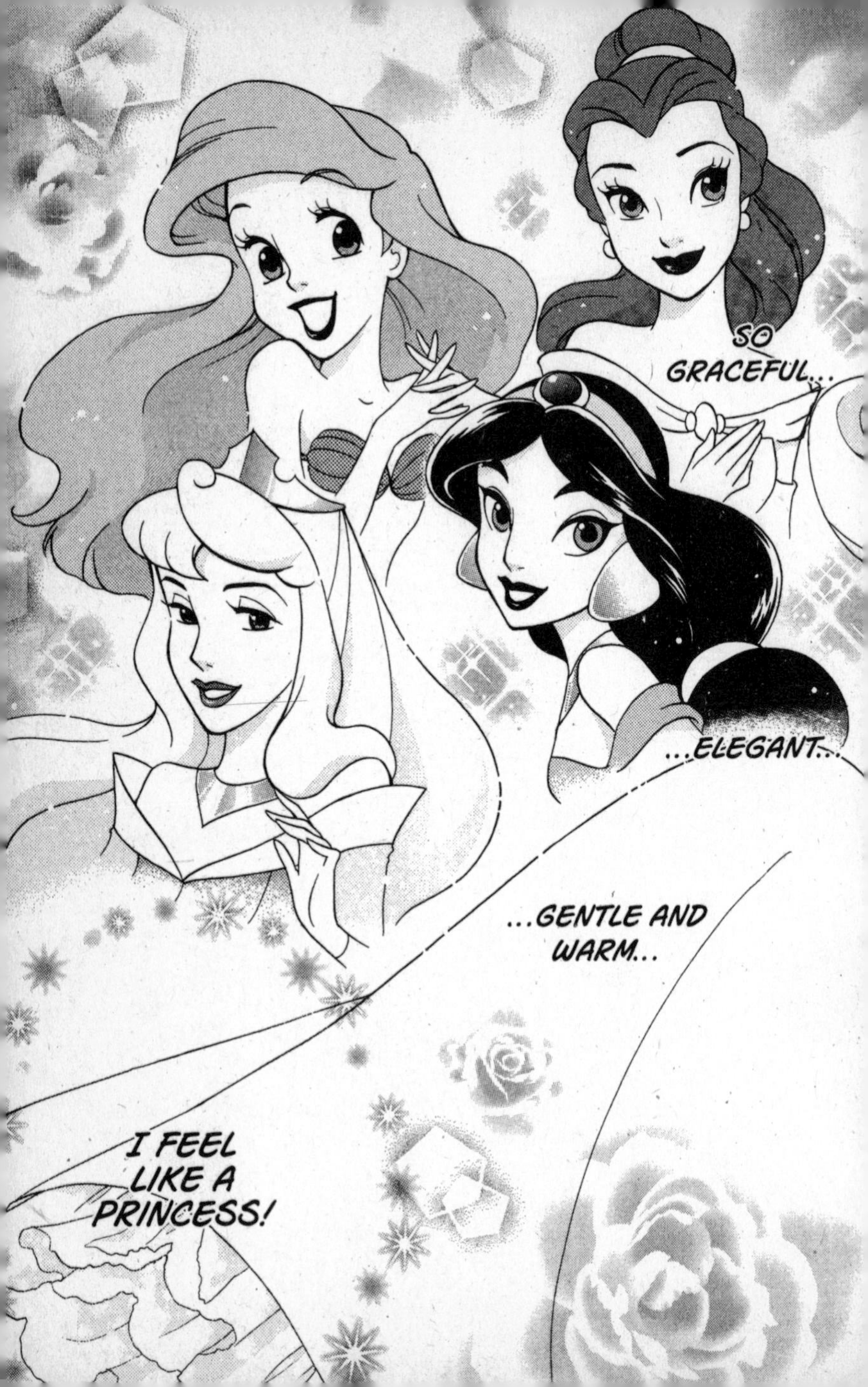
SO GRACEFUL...
...ELEGANT...
...GENTLE AND WARM...
I FEEL LIKE A PRINCESS!

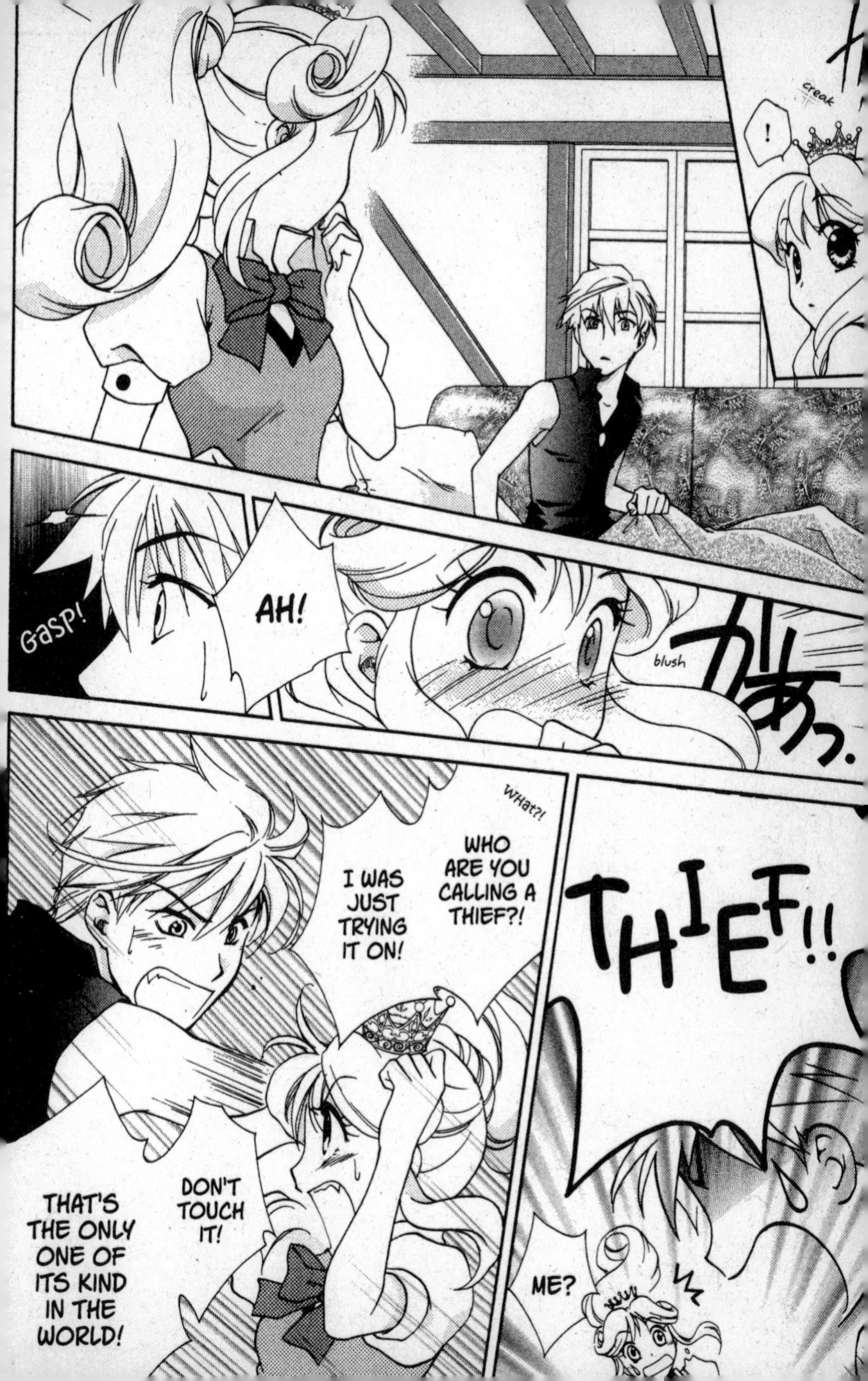
creak
!
blush
かあっ
GASP!
AH!
THIEF!!
ME?
WHAT?!
WHO ARE YOU CALLING A THIEF?!
I WAS JUST TRYING IT ON!
DON'T TOUCH IT!
THAT'S THE ONLY ONE OF ITS KIND IN THE WORLD!

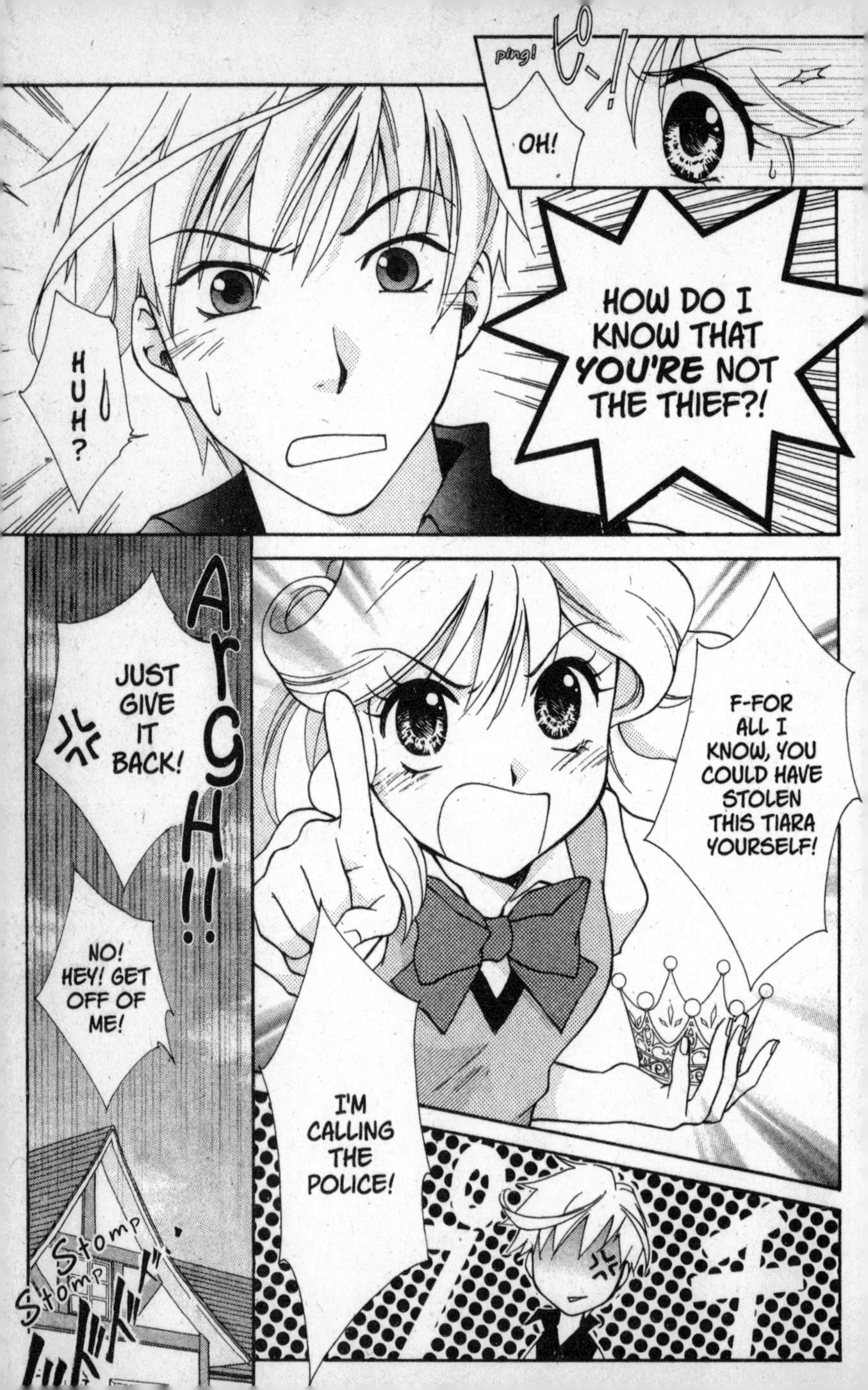

ping!
OH!
HOW DO I KNOW THAT YOU'RE NOT THE THIEF?!
HUH?
F-FOR ALL I KNOW, YOU COULD HAVE STOLEN THIS TIARA YOURSELF!
I'M CALLING THE POLICE!
Argh!!
JUST GIVE IT BACK!
NO! HEY! GET OFF OF ME!
Stomp
Stomp

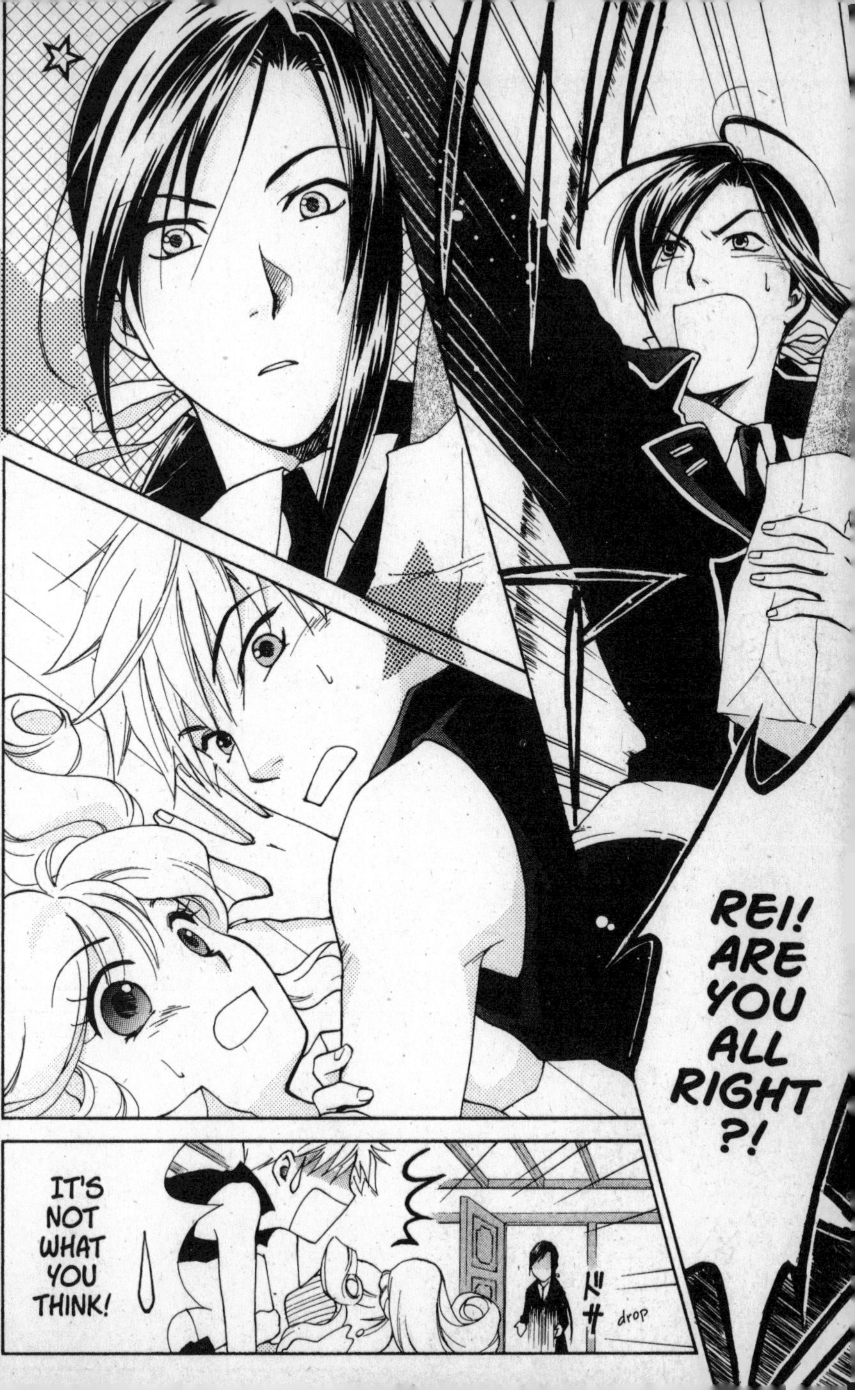
REI! ARE YOU ALL RIGHT?!
ドサ
drop
IT'S NOT WHAT YOU THINK!

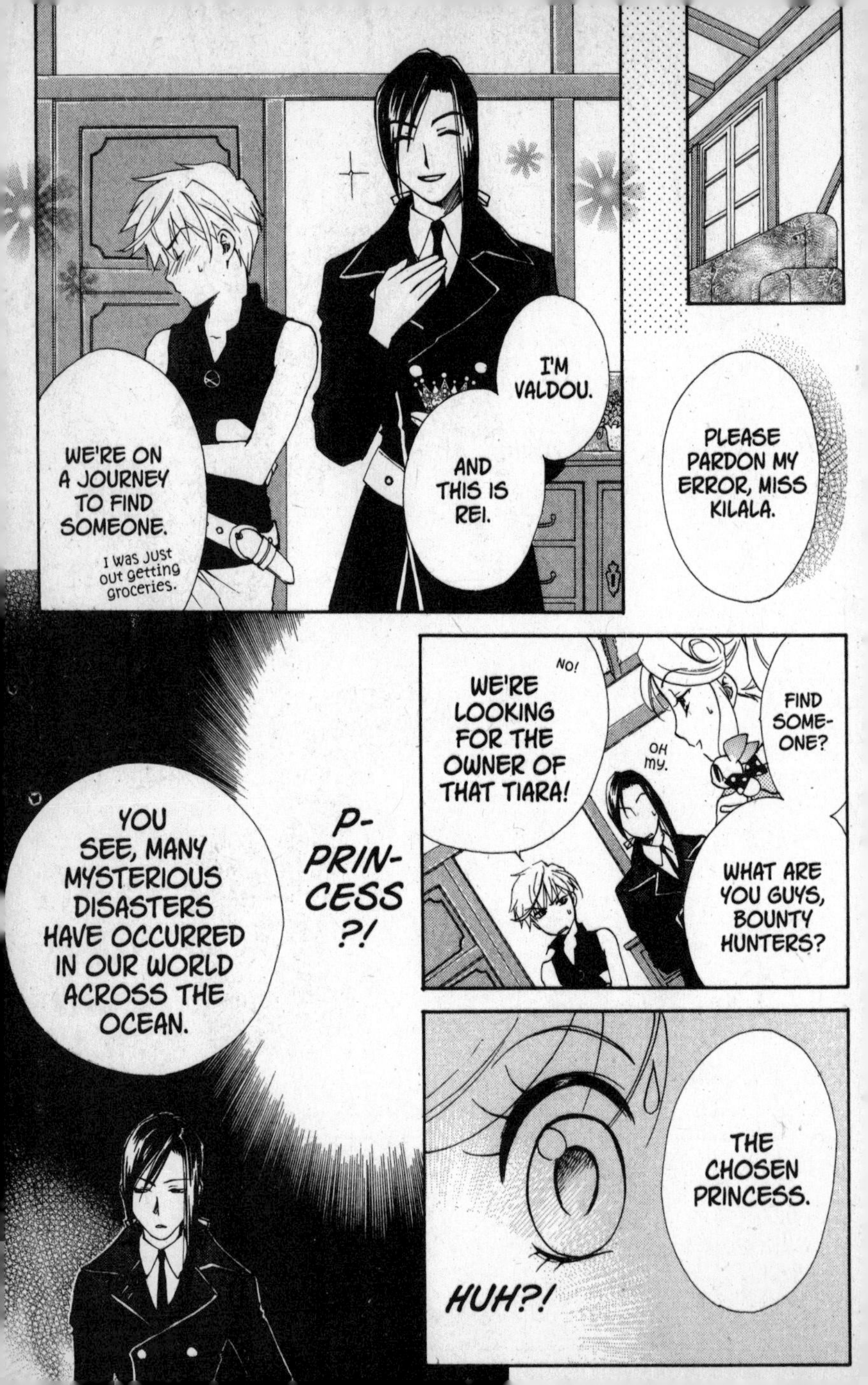
PLEASE PARDON MY ERROR, MISS KILALA.
I'M VALDOU.
AND THIS IS REI.
WE'RE ON A JOURNEY TO FIND SOMEONE.
I was just out getting groceries.
FIND SOME-ONE?
WHAT ARE YOU GUYS, BOUNTY HUNTERS?
OH my.
NO!
WE'RE LOOKING FOR THE OWNER OF THAT TIARA!
THE CHOSEN PRINCESS.
HUH?!
P-PRIN-CESS?!
YOU SEE, MANY MYSTERIOUS DISASTERS HAVE OCCURRED IN OUR WORLD ACROSS THE OCEAN.

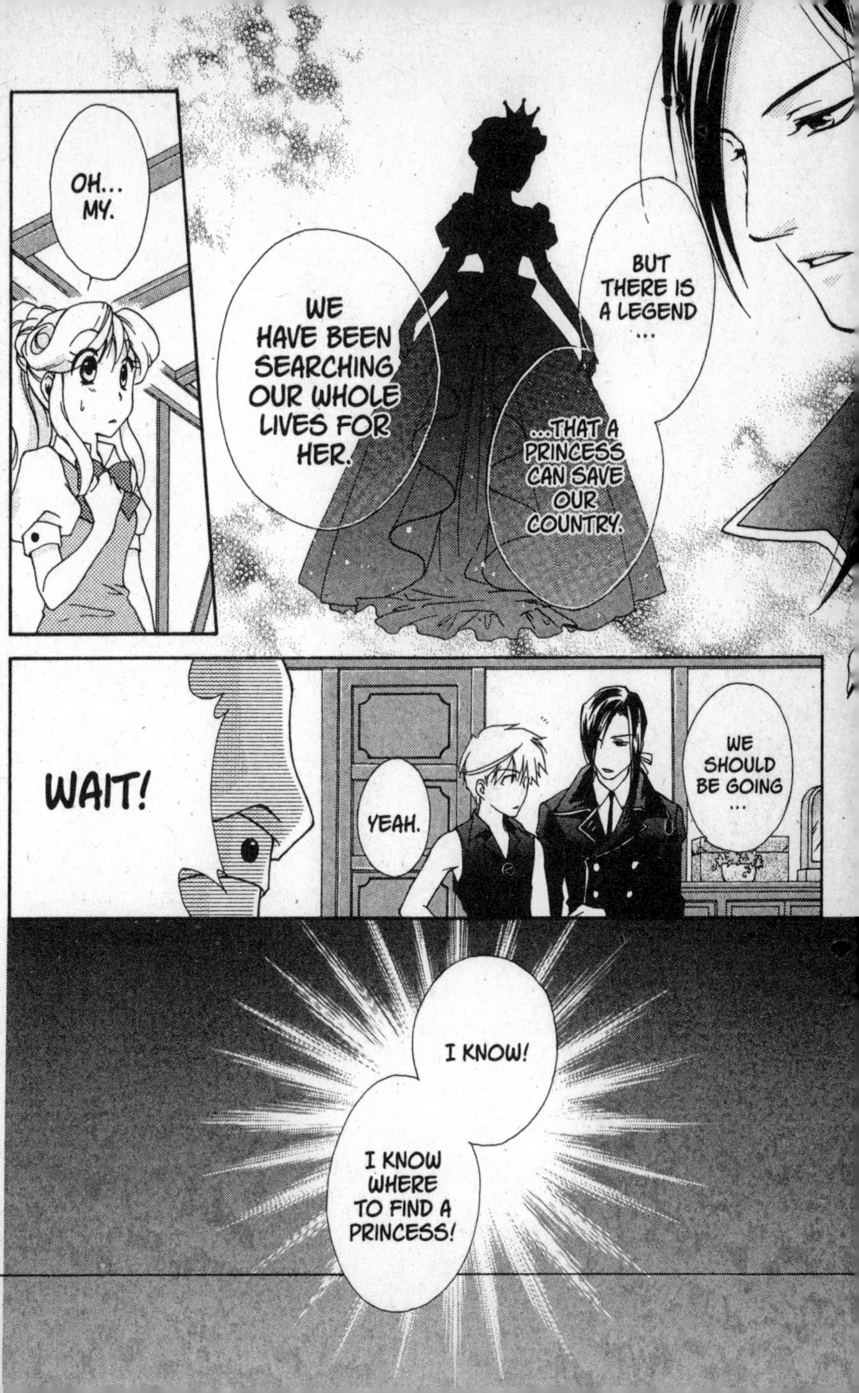
BUT THERE IS A LEGEND ...
...THAT A PRINCESS CAN SAVE OUR COUNTRY.
WE HAVE BEEN SEARCHING OUR WHOLE LIVES FOR HER.
OH... MY.
WE SHOULD BE GOING ...
YEAH.
WAIT!
I KNOW!
I KNOW WHERE TO FIND A PRINCESS!

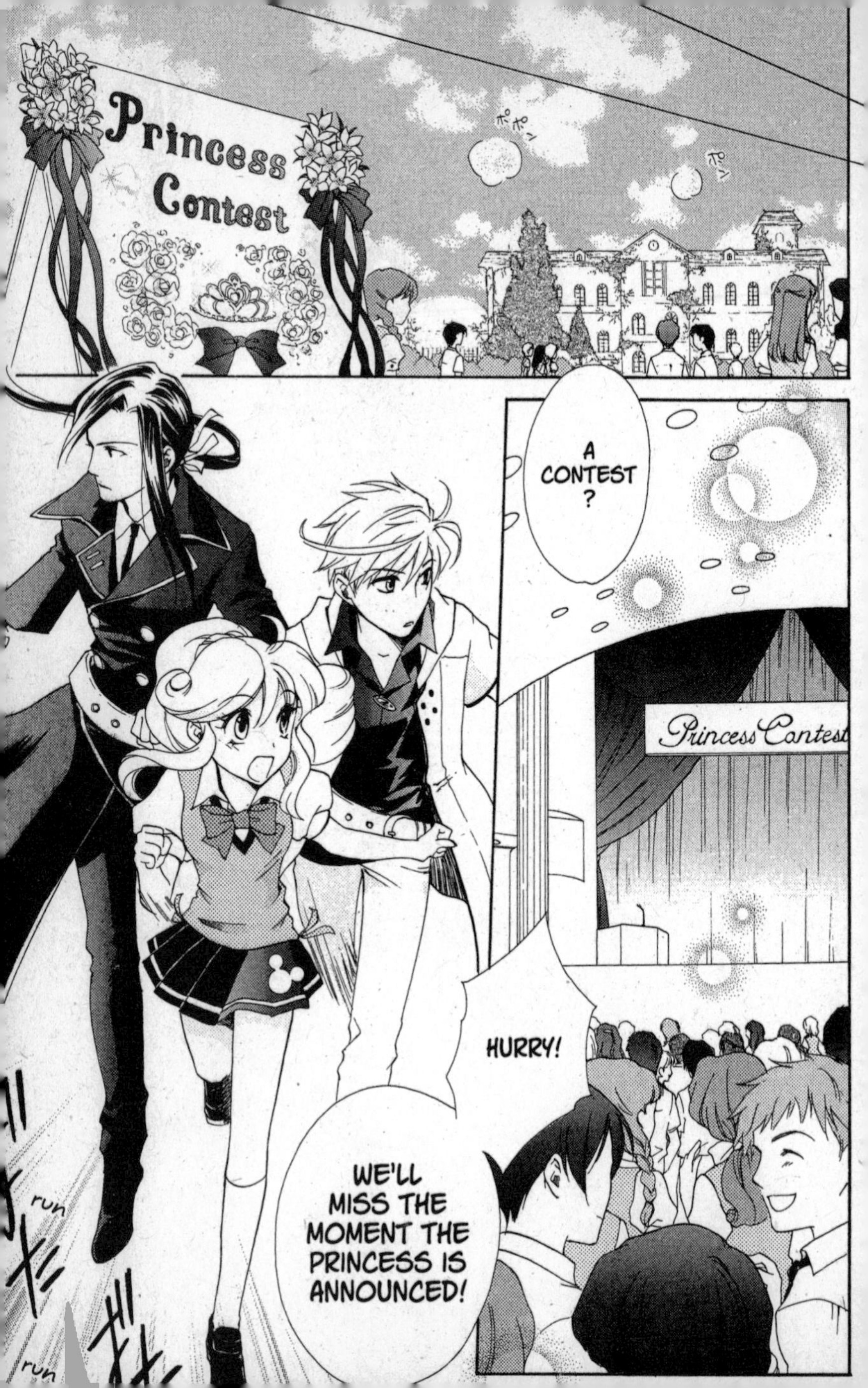
Princess Contest
A CONTEST?
Princess Contest
HURRY!
WE'LL MISS THE MOMENT THE PRINCESS IS ANNOUNCED!
run
run

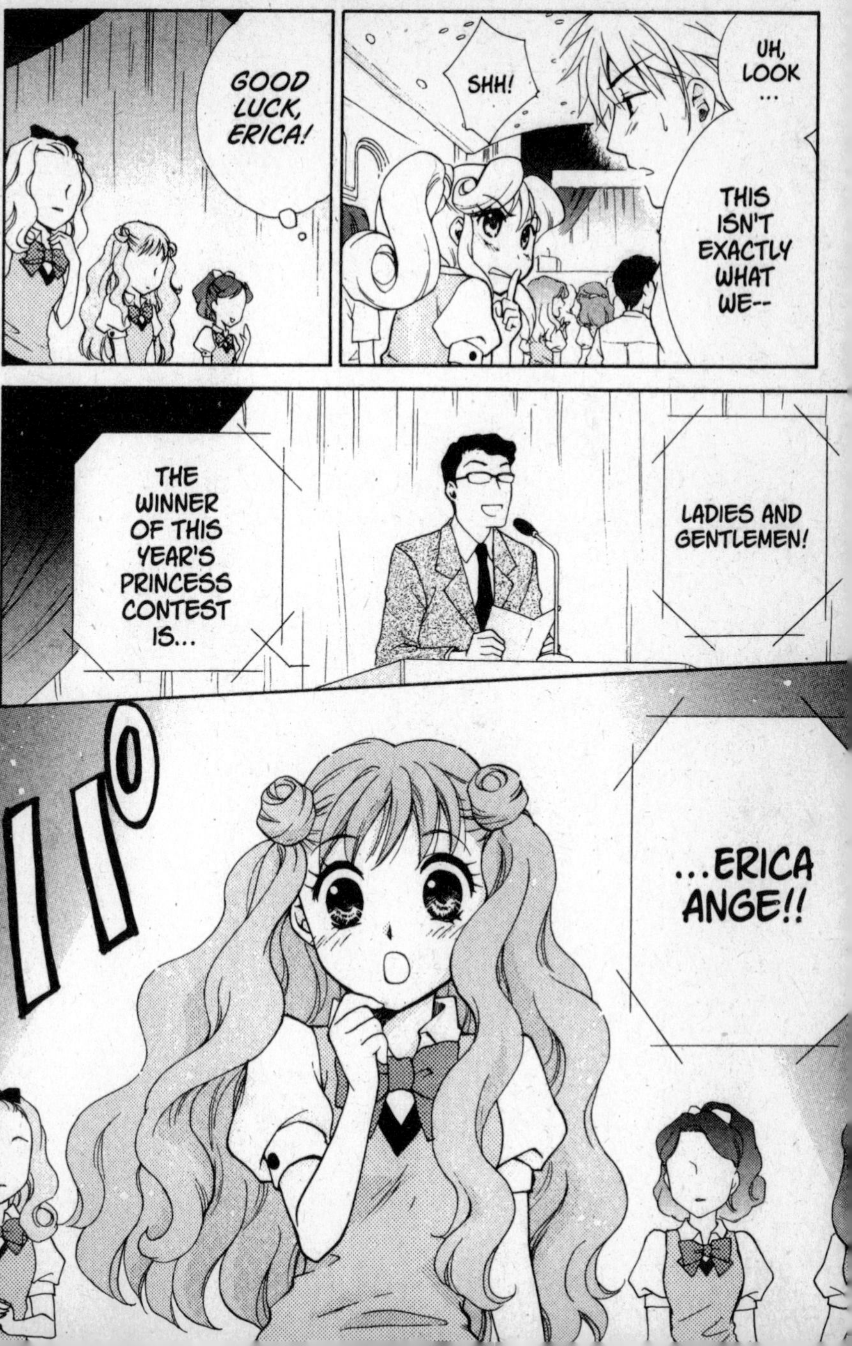
UH, LOOK ...
THIS ISN'T EXACTLY WHAT WE--
SHH!
GOOD LUCK, ERICA!
LADIES AND GENTLEMEN!
THE WINNER OF THIS YEAR'S PRINCESS CONTEST IS...
...ERICA ANGE!!

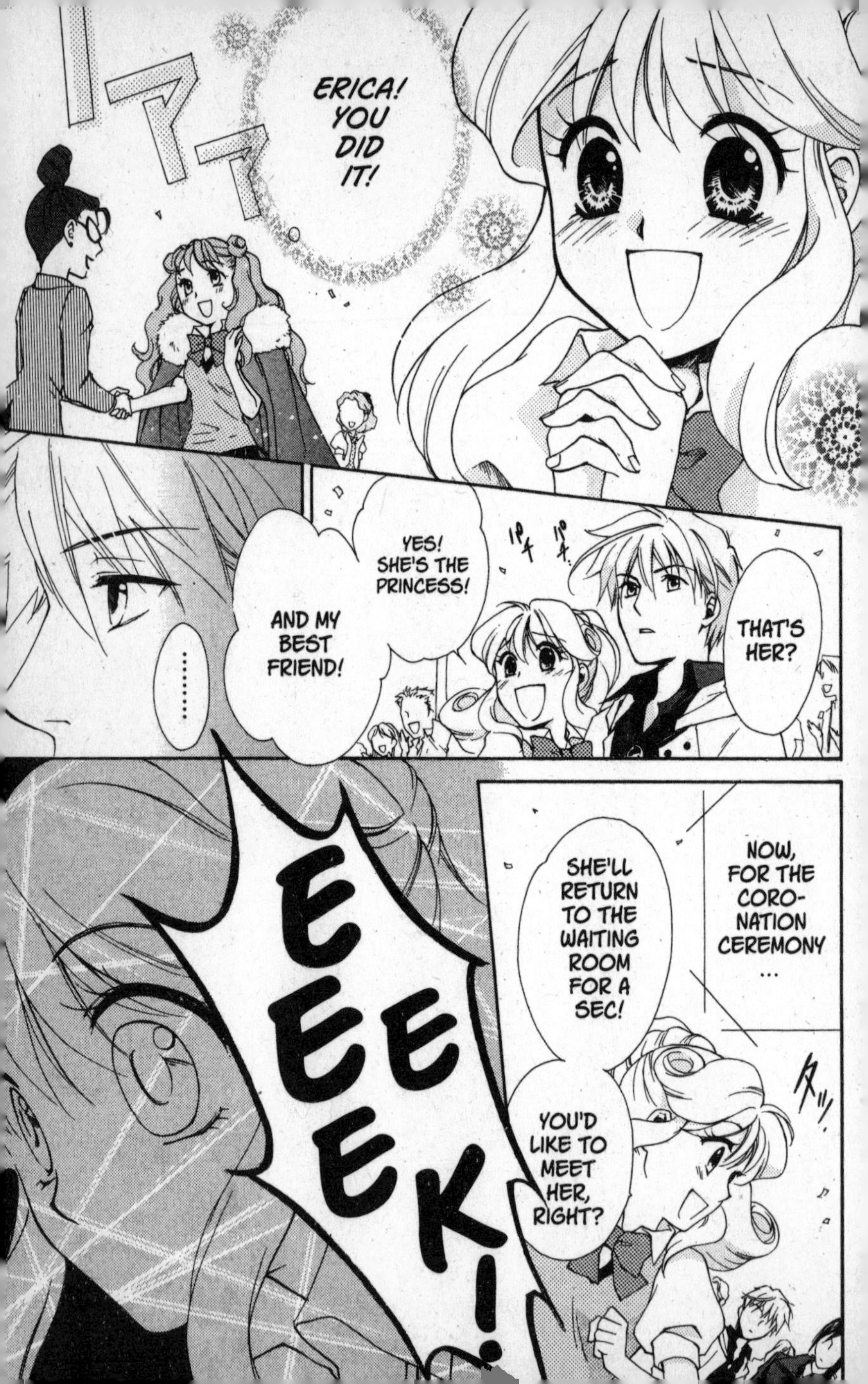
ERICA! YOU DID IT!
THAT'S HER?
YES! SHE'S THE PRINCESS!
AND MY BEST FRIEND!
......
NOW, FOR THE CORO-NATION CEREMONY ...
SHE'LL RETURN TO THE WAITING ROOM FOR A SEC!
YOU'D LIKE TO MEET HER, RIGHT?
EEEEK!

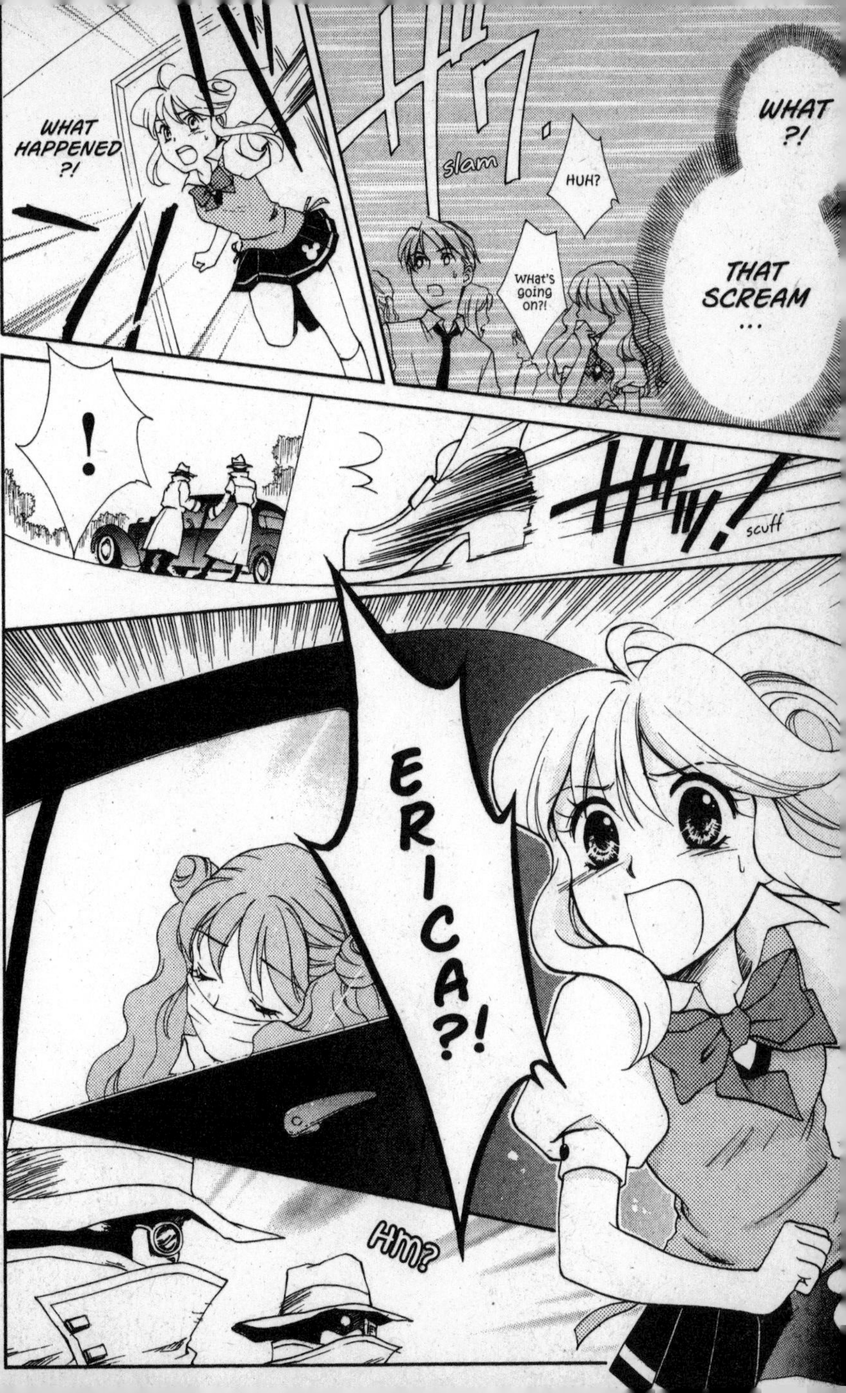
WHAT ?! THAT SCREAM ...
HUH?
slam
What's going on?!
WHAT HAPPENED ?!
scuff
!
ERICA?!
HM?

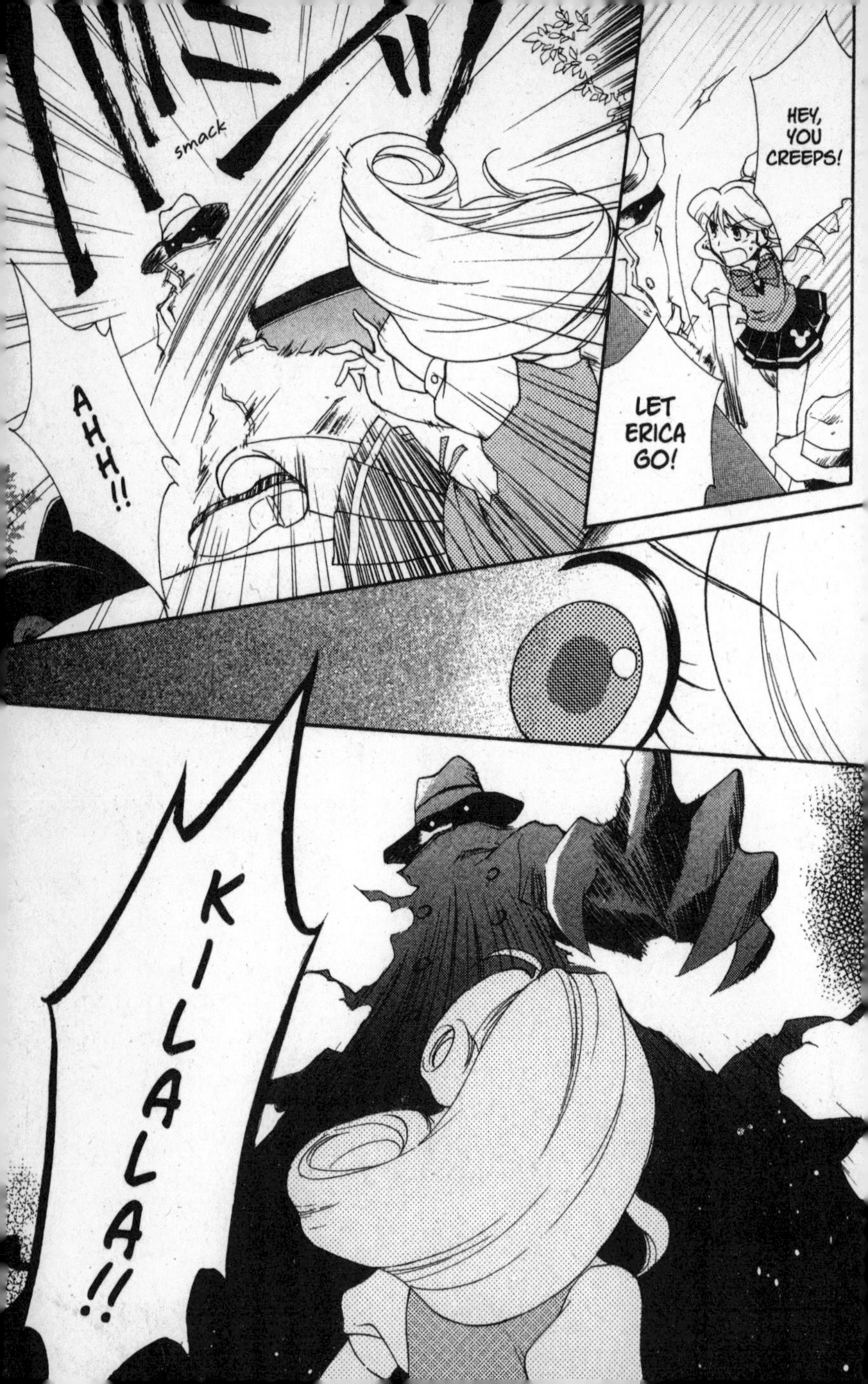
HEY, YOU CREEPS!
LET ERICA GO!
smack
AHH!!
KILALA!!

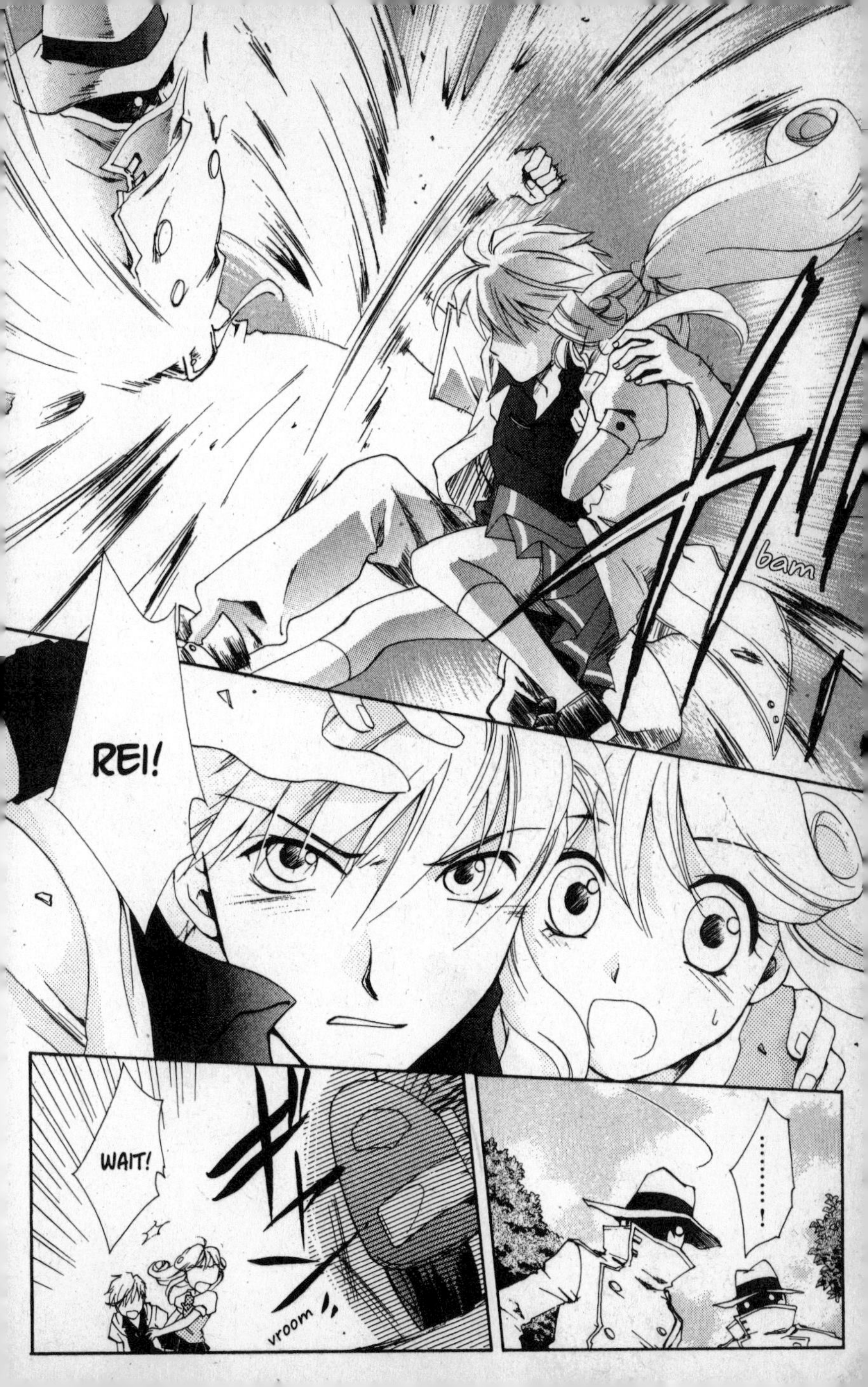
bam
REI!
......!
vroom
WAIT!

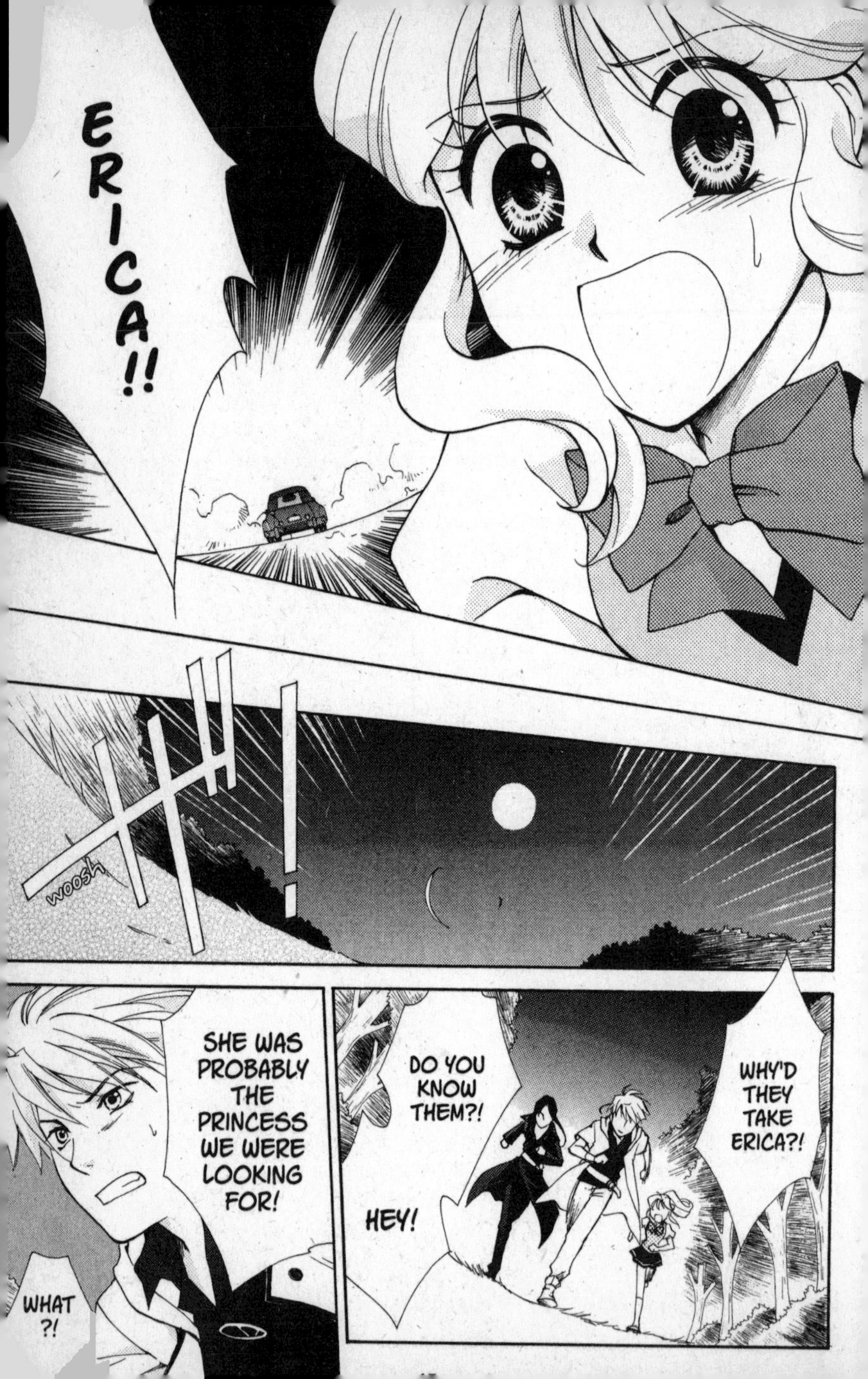
ERICA!!
woosh
!
WHY'D THEY TAKE ERICA?!
DO YOU KNOW THEM?!
HEY!
SHE WAS PROBABLY THE PRINCESS WE WERE LOOKING FOR!
WHAT?!

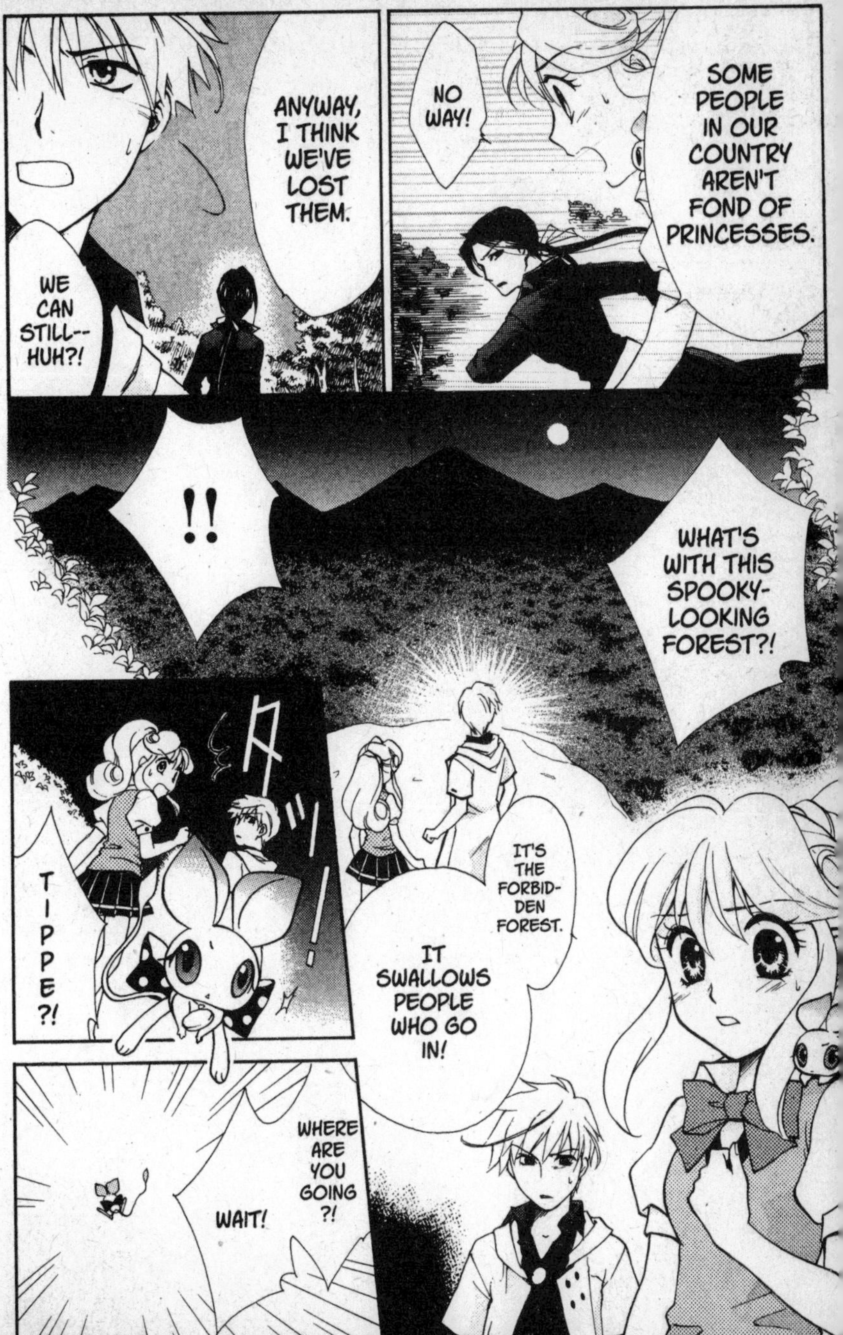
SOME PEOPLE IN OUR COUNTRY AREN'T FOND OF PRINCESSES.
NO WAY!
ANYWAY, I THINK WE'VE LOST THEM.
WE CAN STILL-- HUH?!
!!
WHAT'S WITH THIS SPOOKY-LOOKING FOREST?!
IT'S THE FORBIDDEN FOREST.
IT SWALLOWS PEOPLE WHO GO IN!
TIPPE?!
WHERE ARE YOU GOING?!
WAIT!

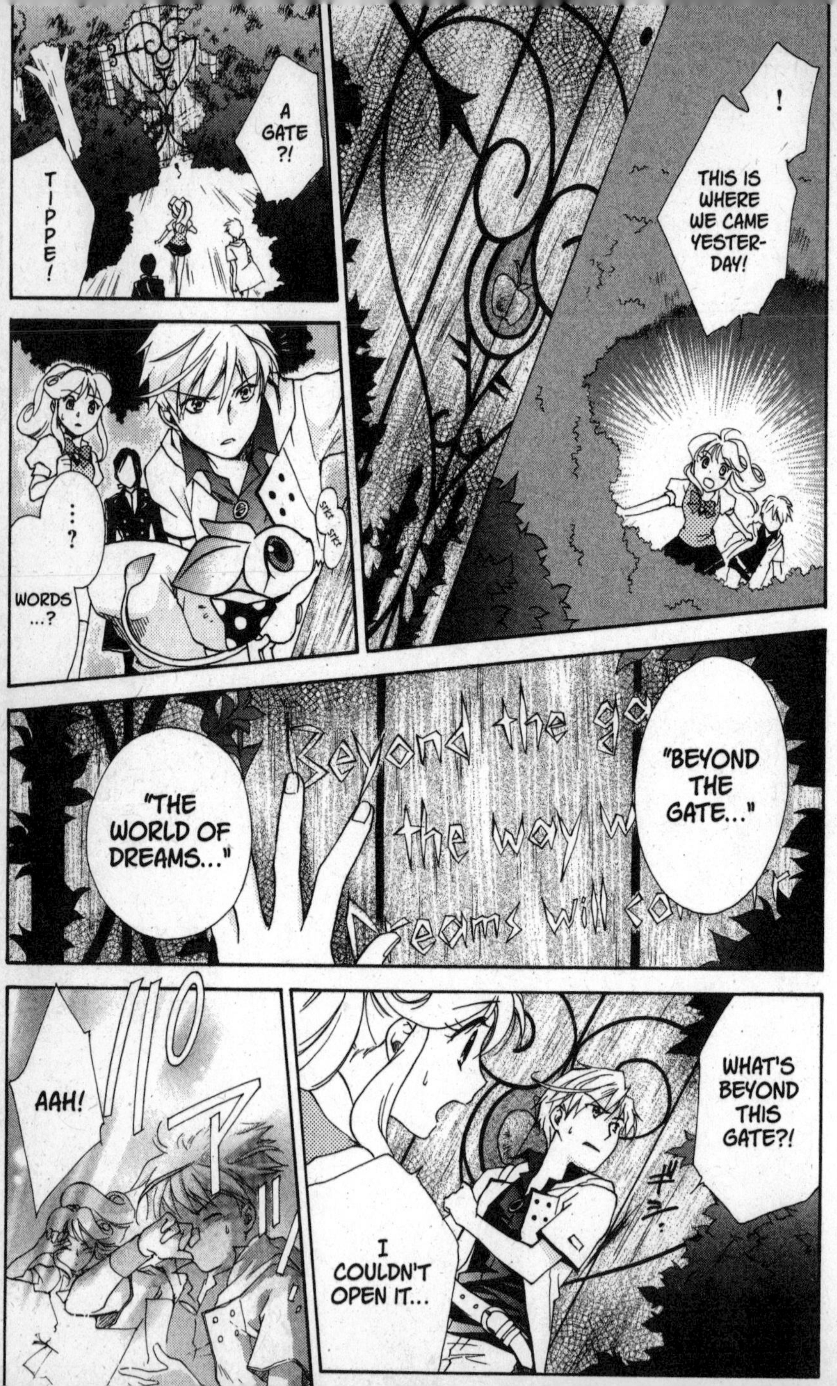
!
THIS IS WHERE WE CAME YESTER-DAY!
A GATE?!
TIPPE!
...?
WORDS...?
"BEYOND THE GATE..."
"THE WORLD OF DREAMS..."
WHAT'S BEYOND THIS GATE?!
I COULDN'T OPEN IT...
AAH!

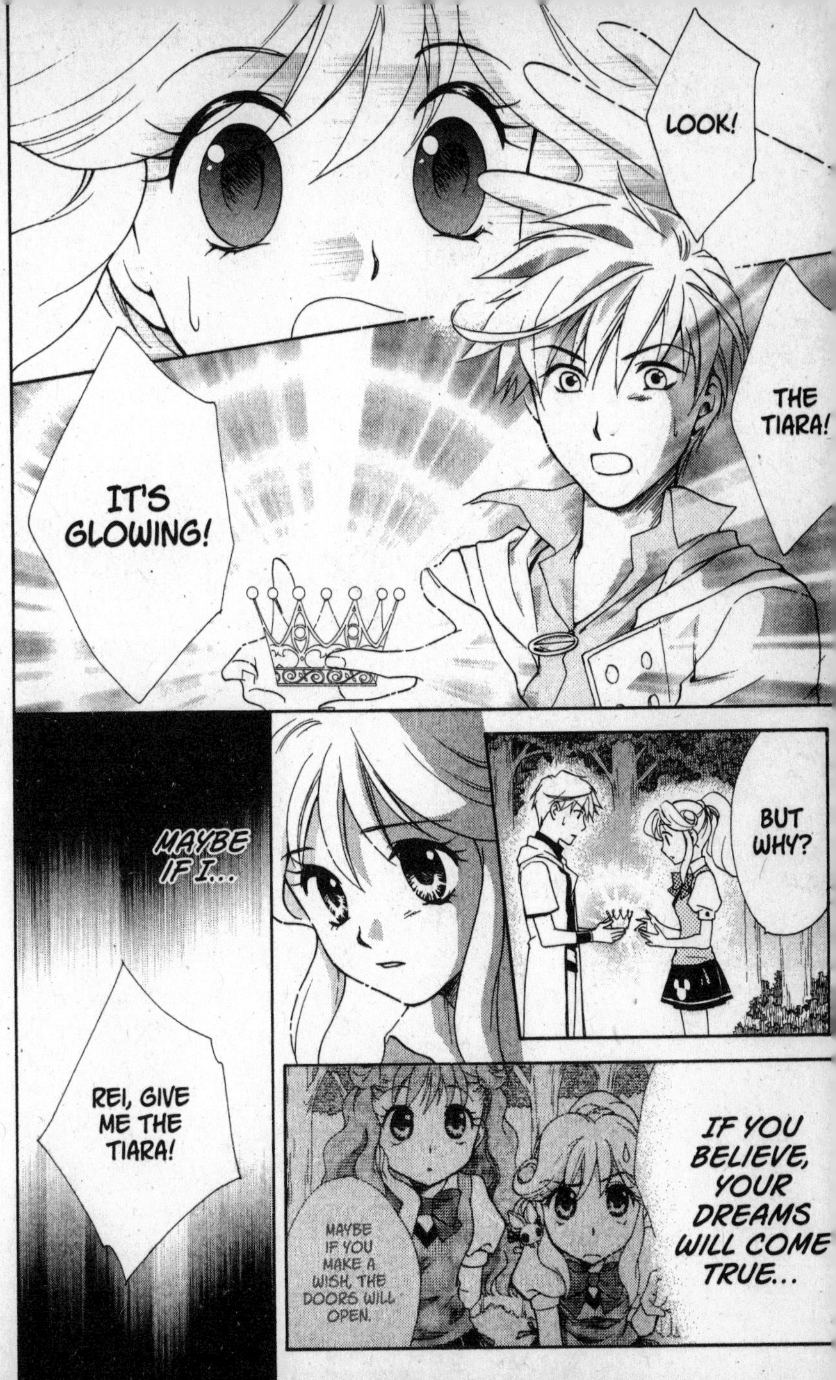
LOOK!
THE TIARA!
IT'S GLOWING!
BUT WHY?
MAYBE IF I...
IF YOU BELIEVE, YOUR DREAMS WILL COME TRUE...
MAYBE IF YOU MAKE A WISH, THE DOORS WILL OPEN.
REI, GIVE ME THE TIARA!

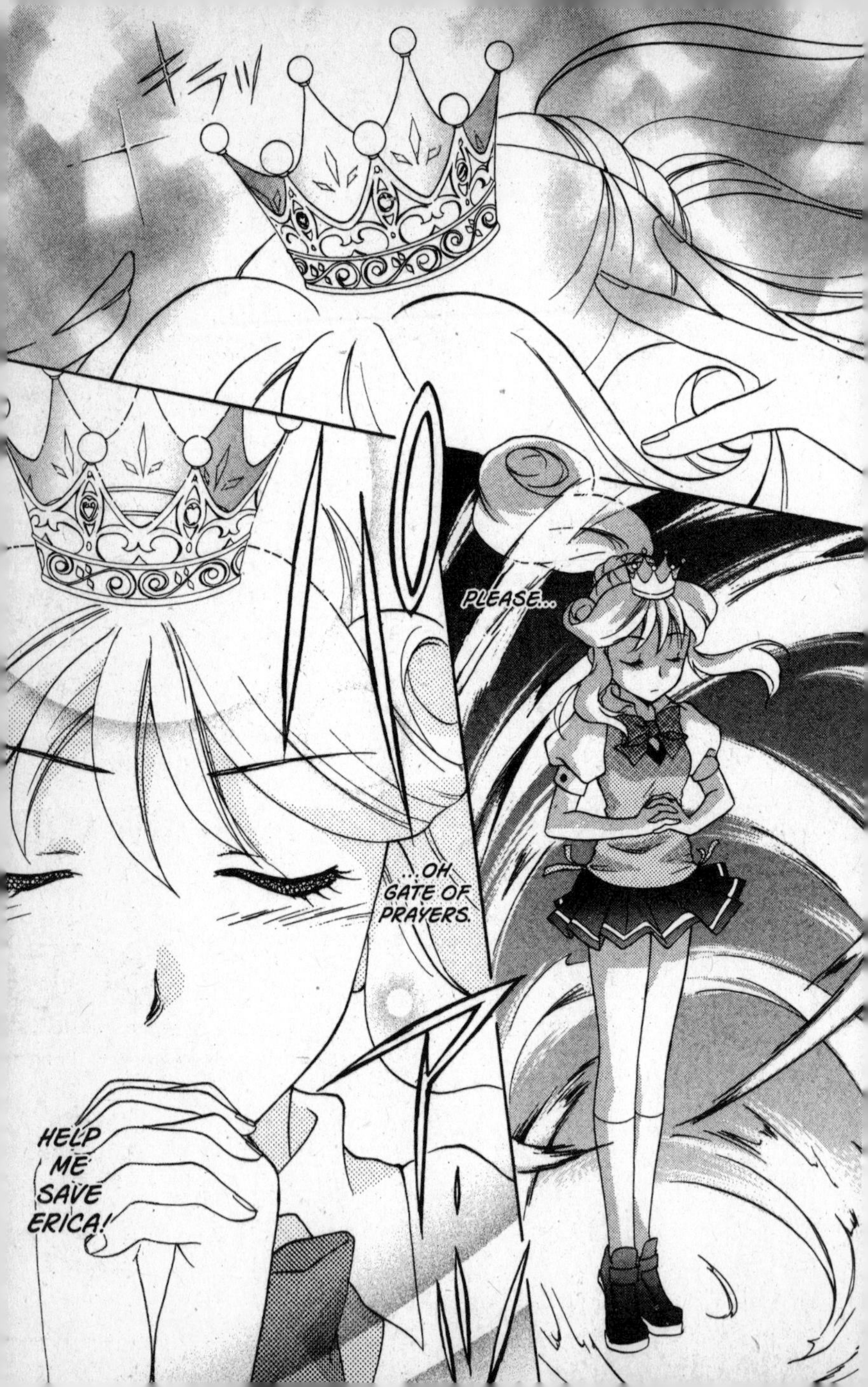
キラッ
PLEASE...
...OH GATE OF PRAYERS.
HELP ME SAVE ERICA!

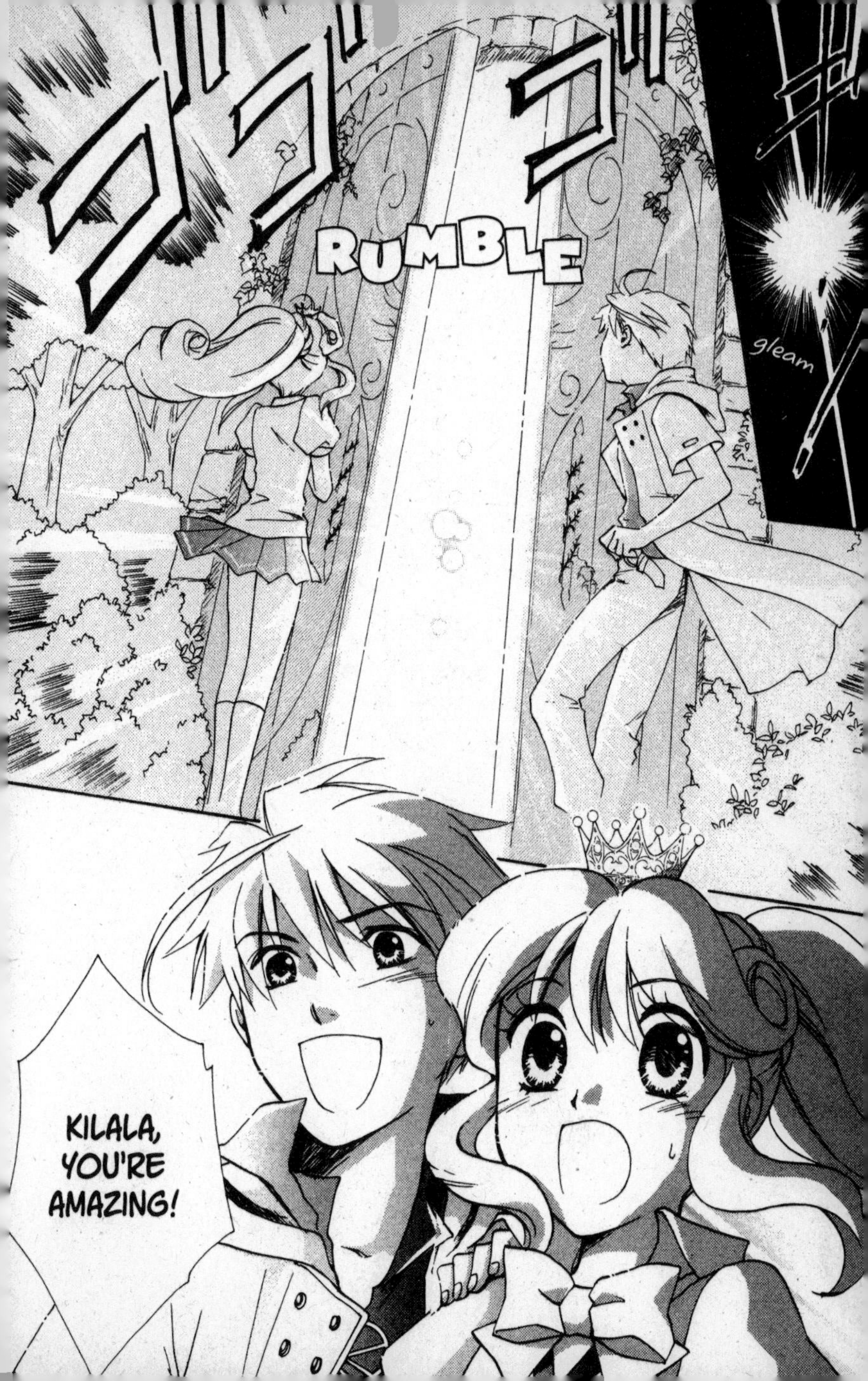
gleam
RUMBLE
KILALA, YOU'RE AMAZING!

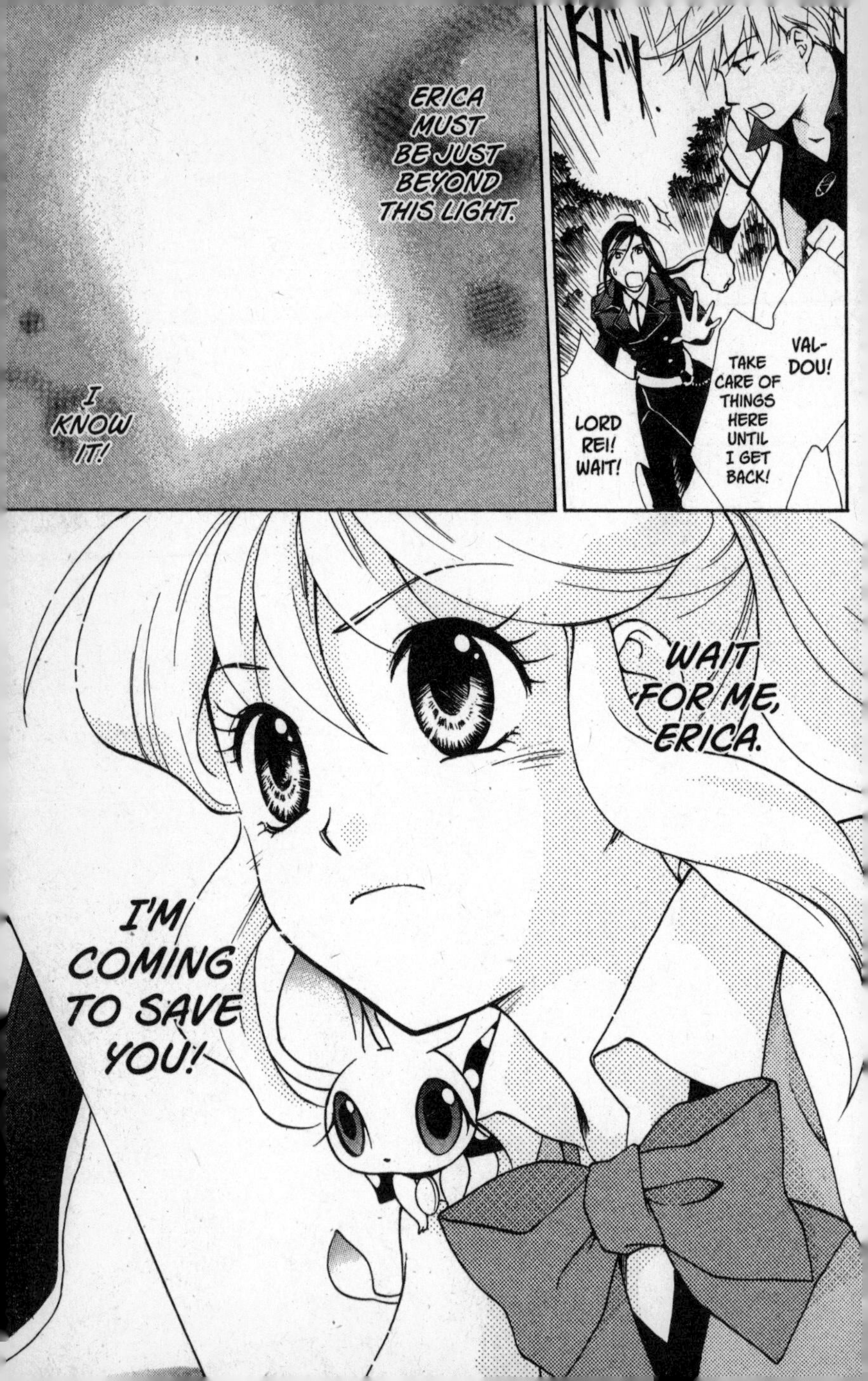
VAL-DOU!
TAKE CARE OF THINGS HERE UNTIL I GET BACK!
LORD REI! WAIT!
ERICA MUST BE JUST BEYOND THIS LIGHT.
I KNOW IT!
WAIT FOR ME, ERICA.
I'M COMING TO SAVE YOU!

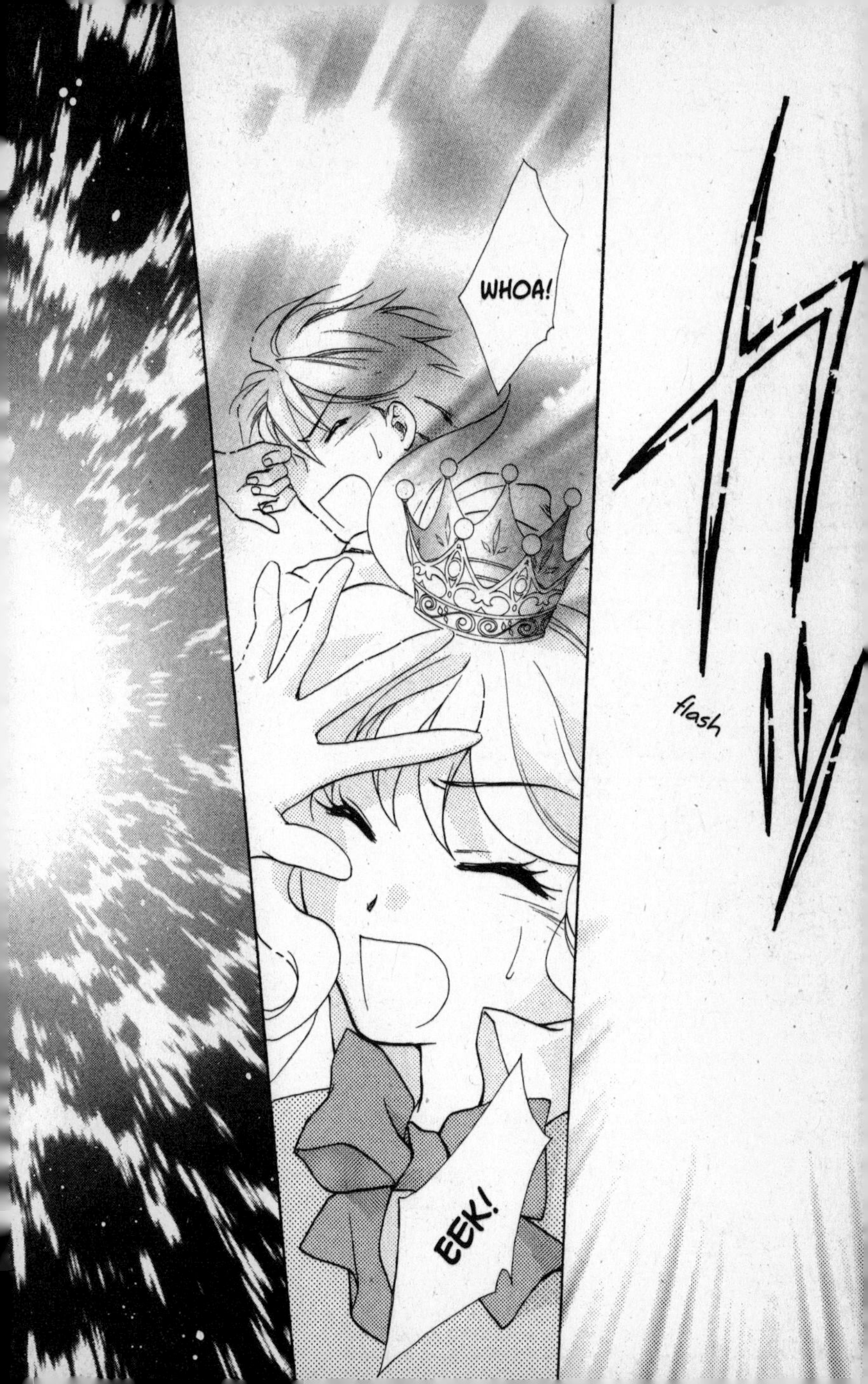
flash
WHOA!
EEK!

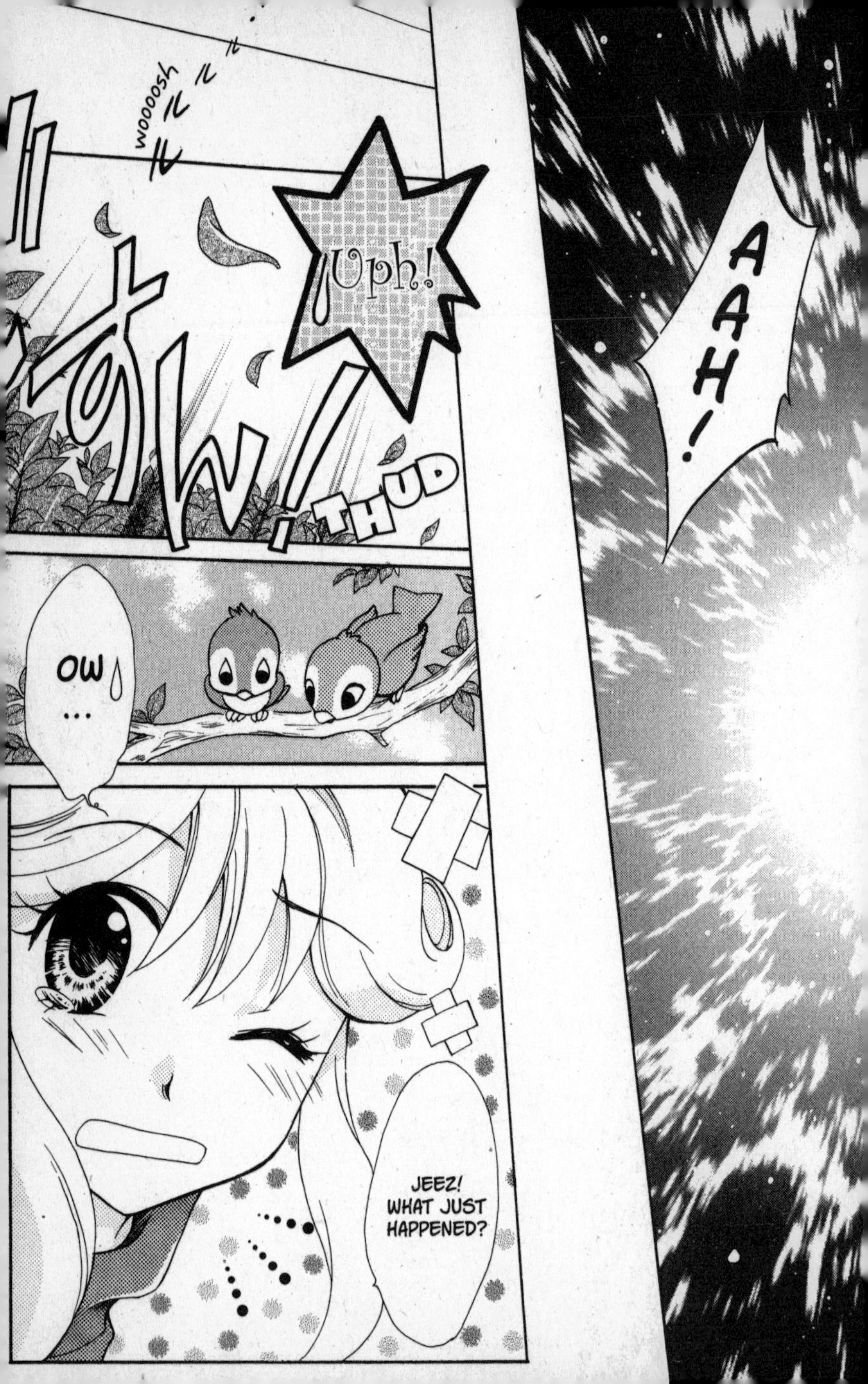
AAH!
wooooosh
Uph!
THUD
OW ...
JEEZ! WHAT JUST HAPPENED?

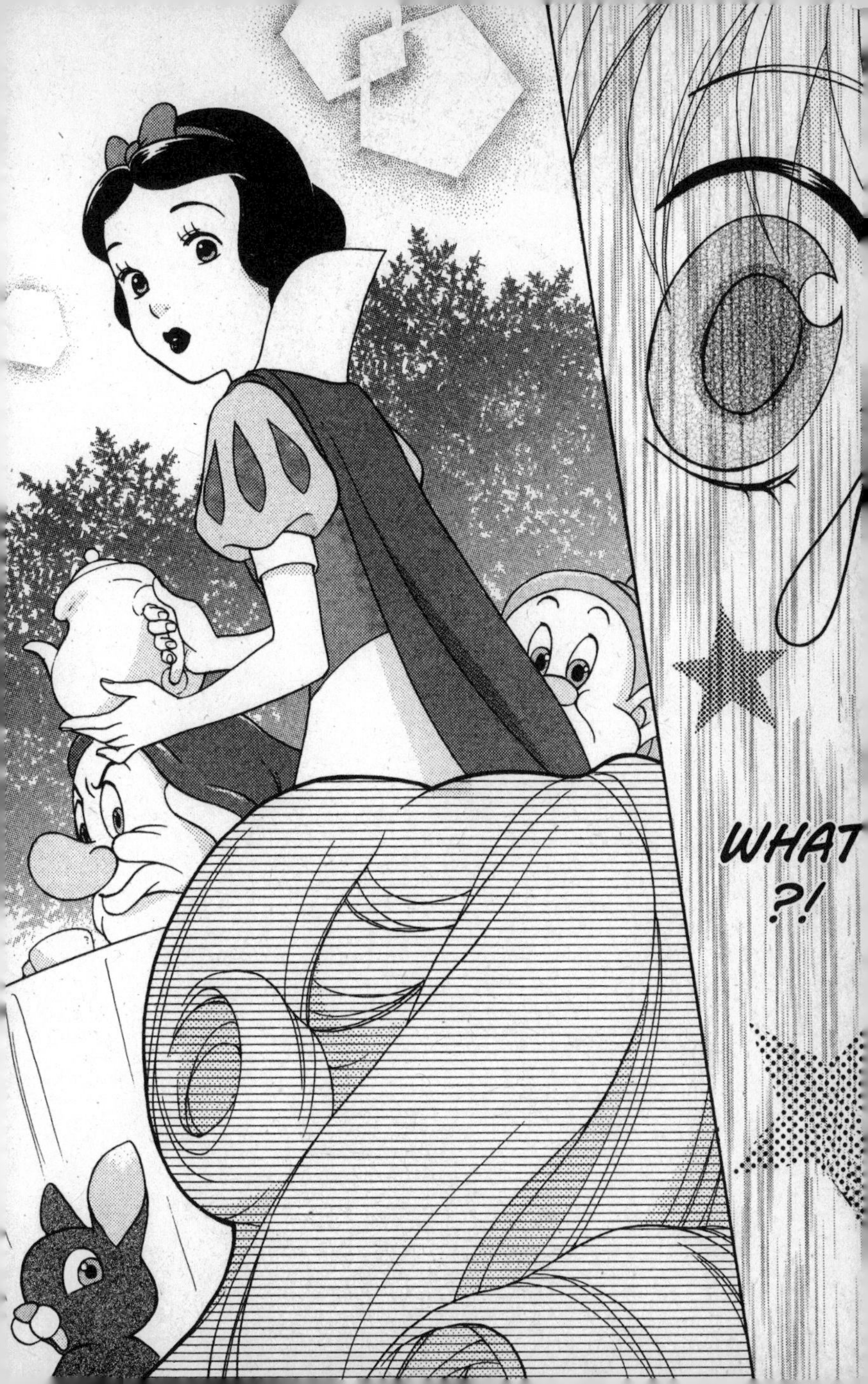
WHAT
?!

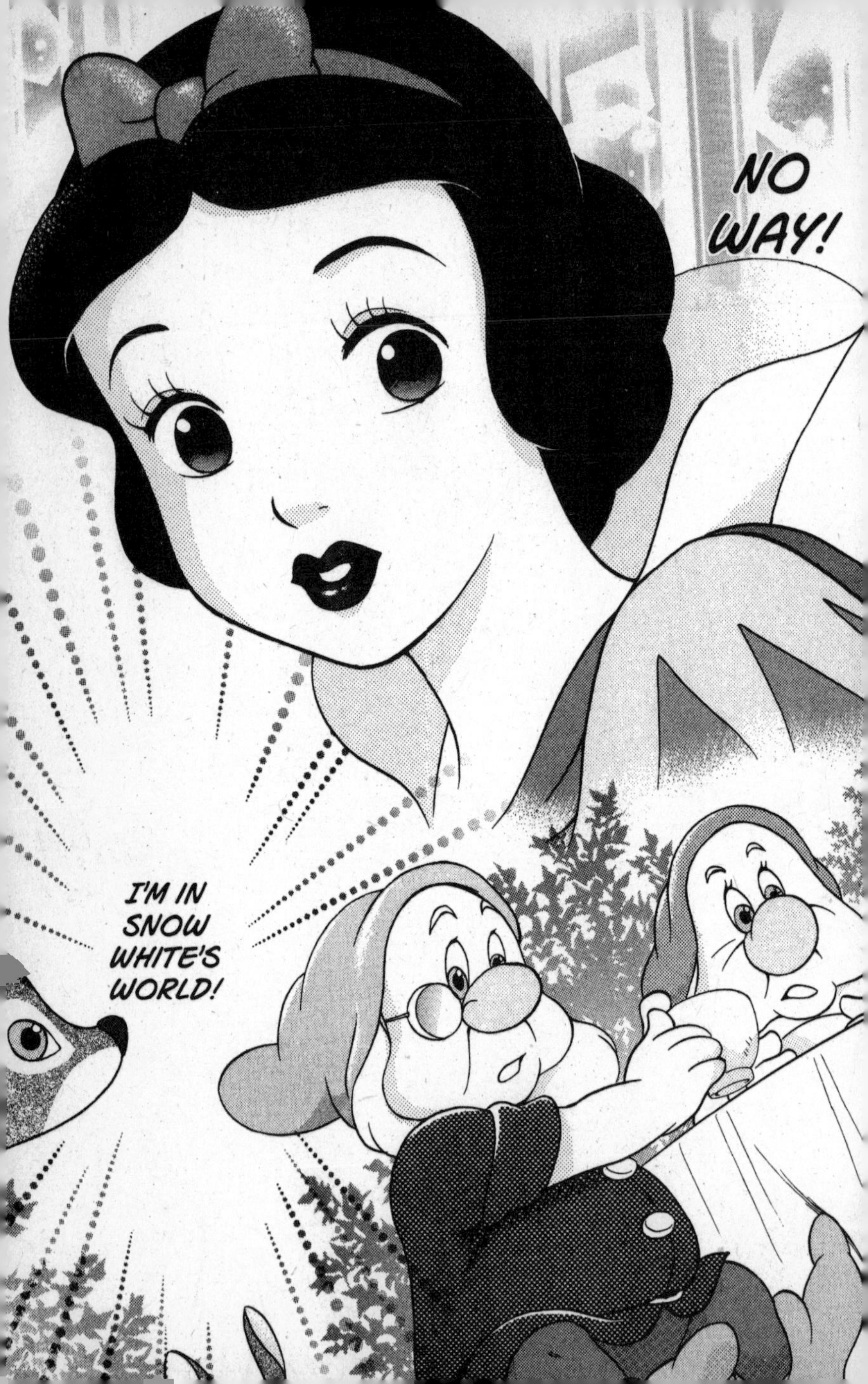
NO WAY!
I'M IN SNOW WHITE'S WORLD!

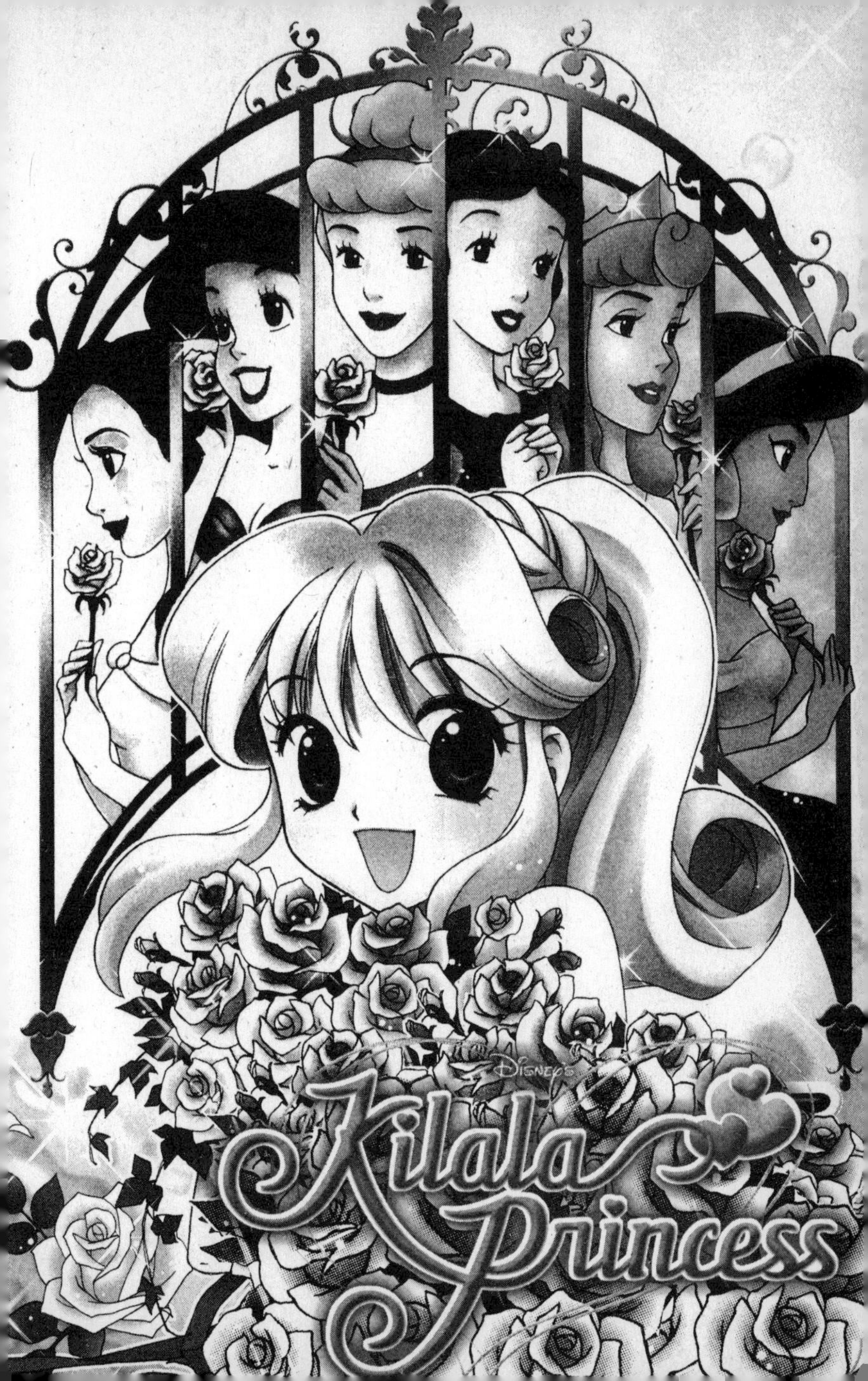
Disney's
Kilala Princess

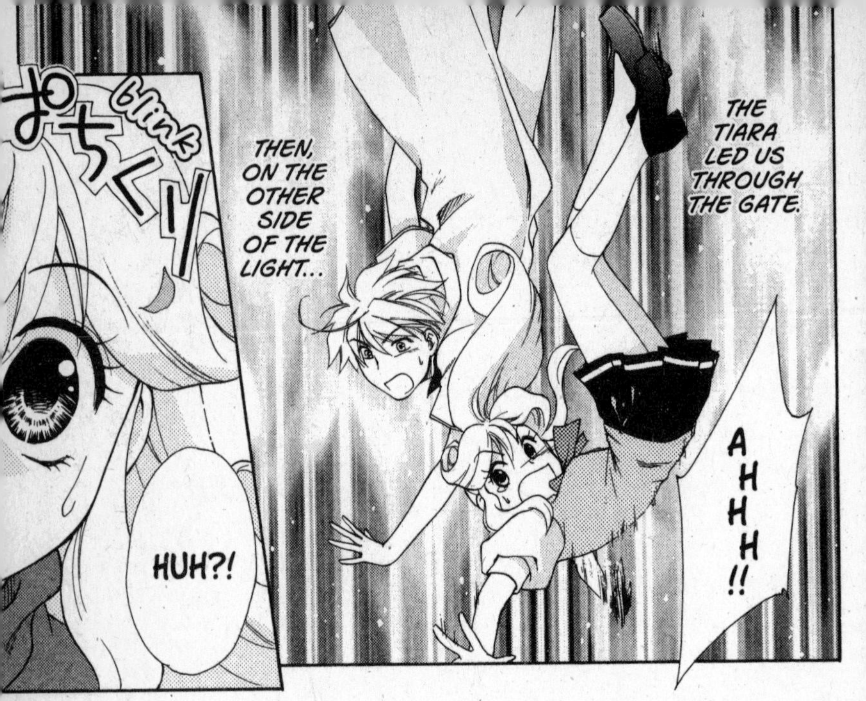
THE TIARA LED US THROUGH THE GATE.
THEN, ON THE OTHER SIDE OF THE LIGHT...
AHHH!!
ぱちくり
blink
HUH?!

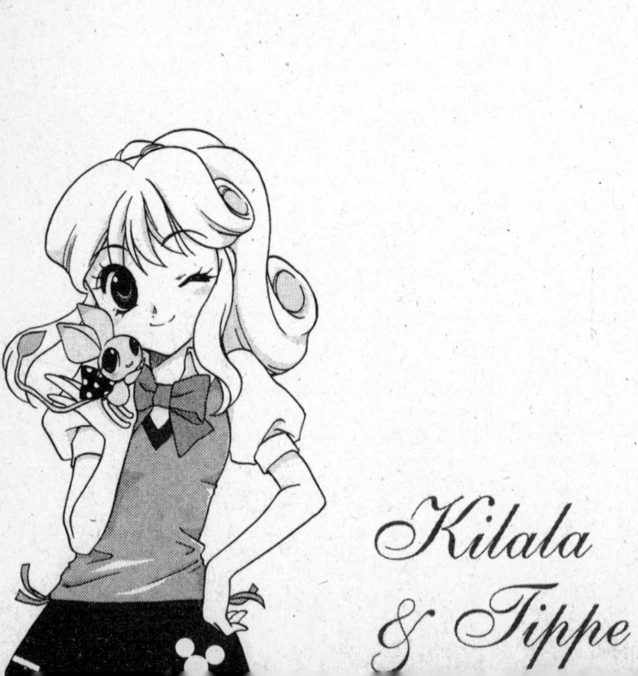
Kilala & Tippe

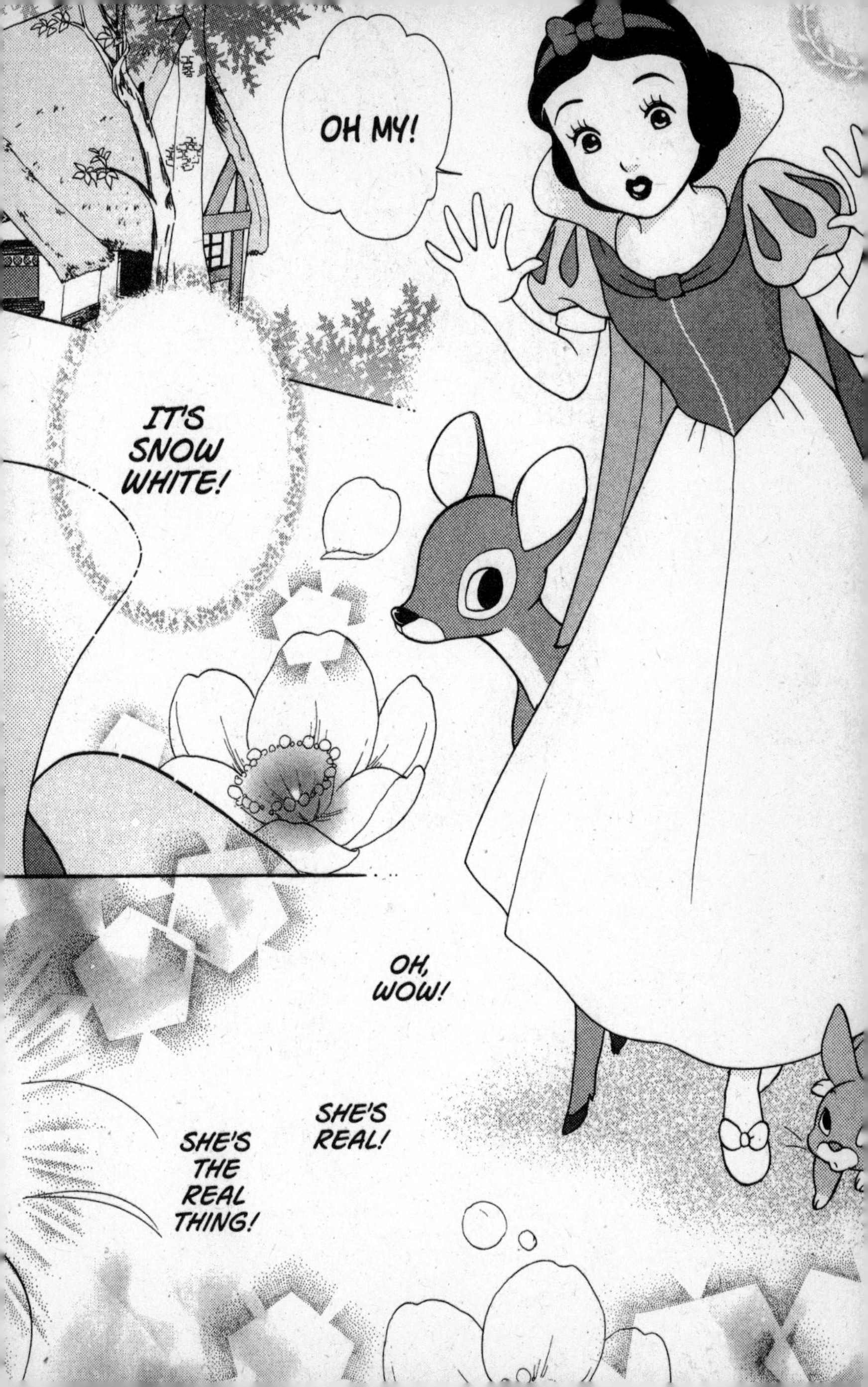
OH MY!
IT'S SNOW WHITE!
OH, WOW!
SHE'S REAL!
SHE'S THE REAL THING!

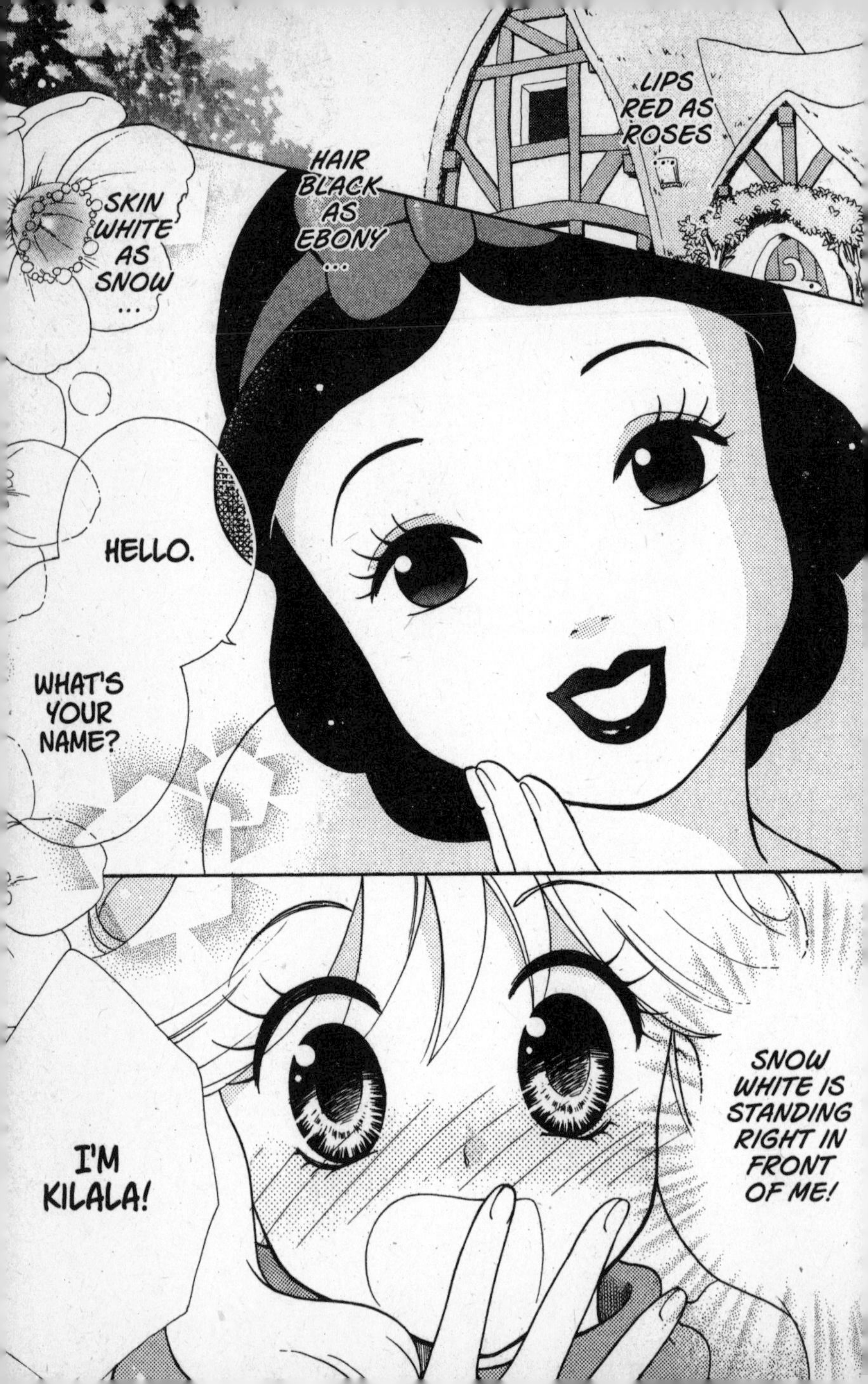
LIPS RED AS ROSES ...
HAIR BLACK AS EBONY ...
SKIN WHITE AS SNOW ...
HELLO.
WHAT'S YOUR NAME?
SNOW WHITE IS STANDING RIGHT IN FRONT OF ME!
I'M KILALA!

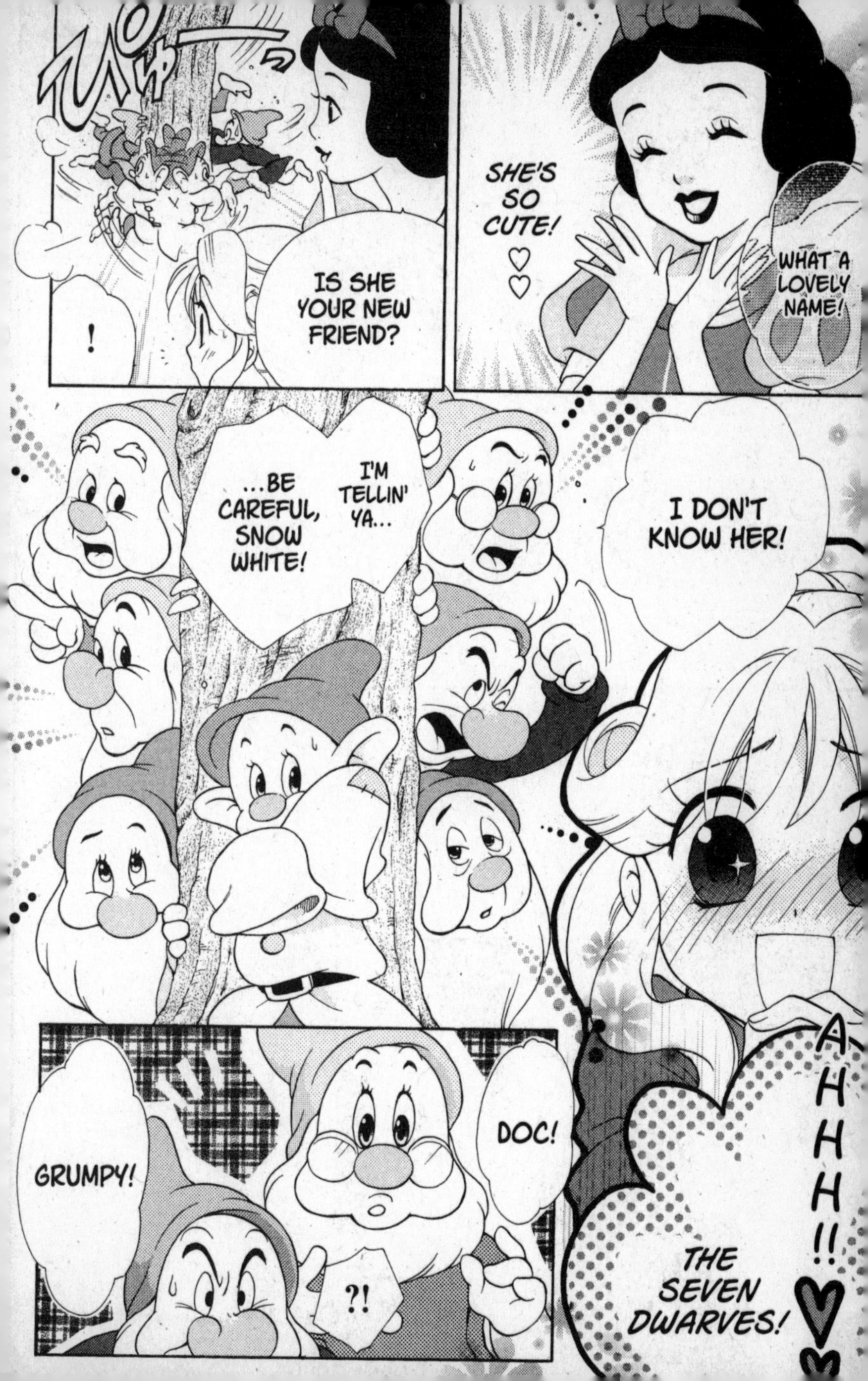
WHAT A LOVELY NAME!
SHE'S SO CUTE! ♡ ♡
IS SHE YOUR NEW FRIEND?
!
I DON'T KNOW HER!
I'M TELLIN' YA...
...BE CAREFUL, SNOW WHITE!
AHHH!! ♡
THE SEVEN DWARVES!
DOC!
GRUMPY!
?!

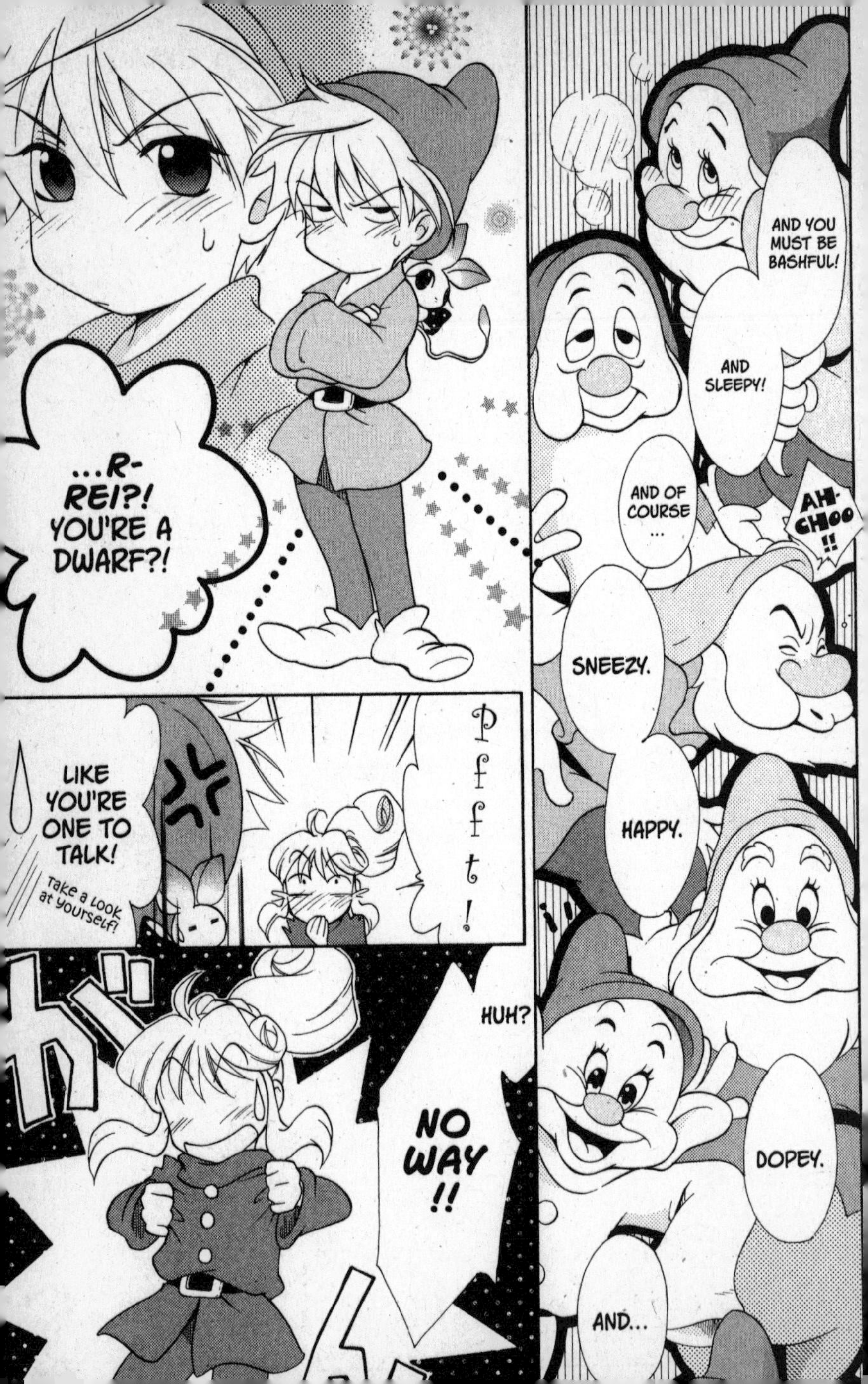
AND YOU MUST BE BASHFUL!
AND SLEEPY!
AH-CHOO!!
AND OF COURSE...
SNEEZY.
HAPPY.
DOPEY.
AND...
...R-REI?! YOU'RE A DWARF?!
Pffft!
LIKE YOU'RE ONE TO TALK!
Take a look at yourself!
HUH?
NO WAY!!

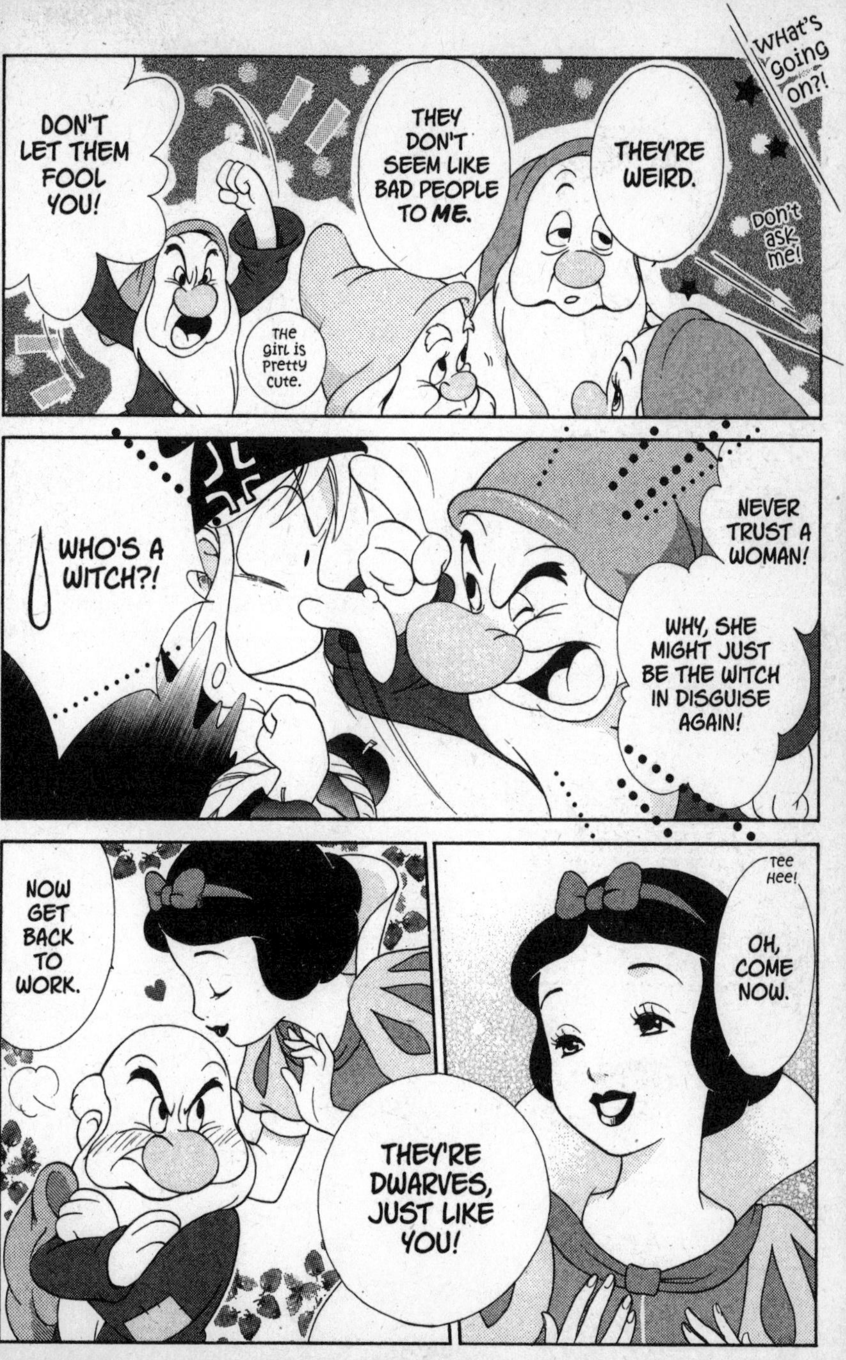
What's going on?!
THEY'RE WEIRD.
Don't ask me!
THEY DON'T SEEM LIKE BAD PEOPLE TO ME.
DON'T LET THEM FOOL YOU!
The girl is pretty cute.
NEVER TRUST A WOMAN!
WHY, SHE MIGHT JUST BE THE WITCH IN DISGUISE AGAIN!
WHO'S A WITCH?!
Tee Hee!
OH, COME NOW.
THEY'RE DWARVES, JUST LIKE YOU!
NOW GET BACK TO WORK.

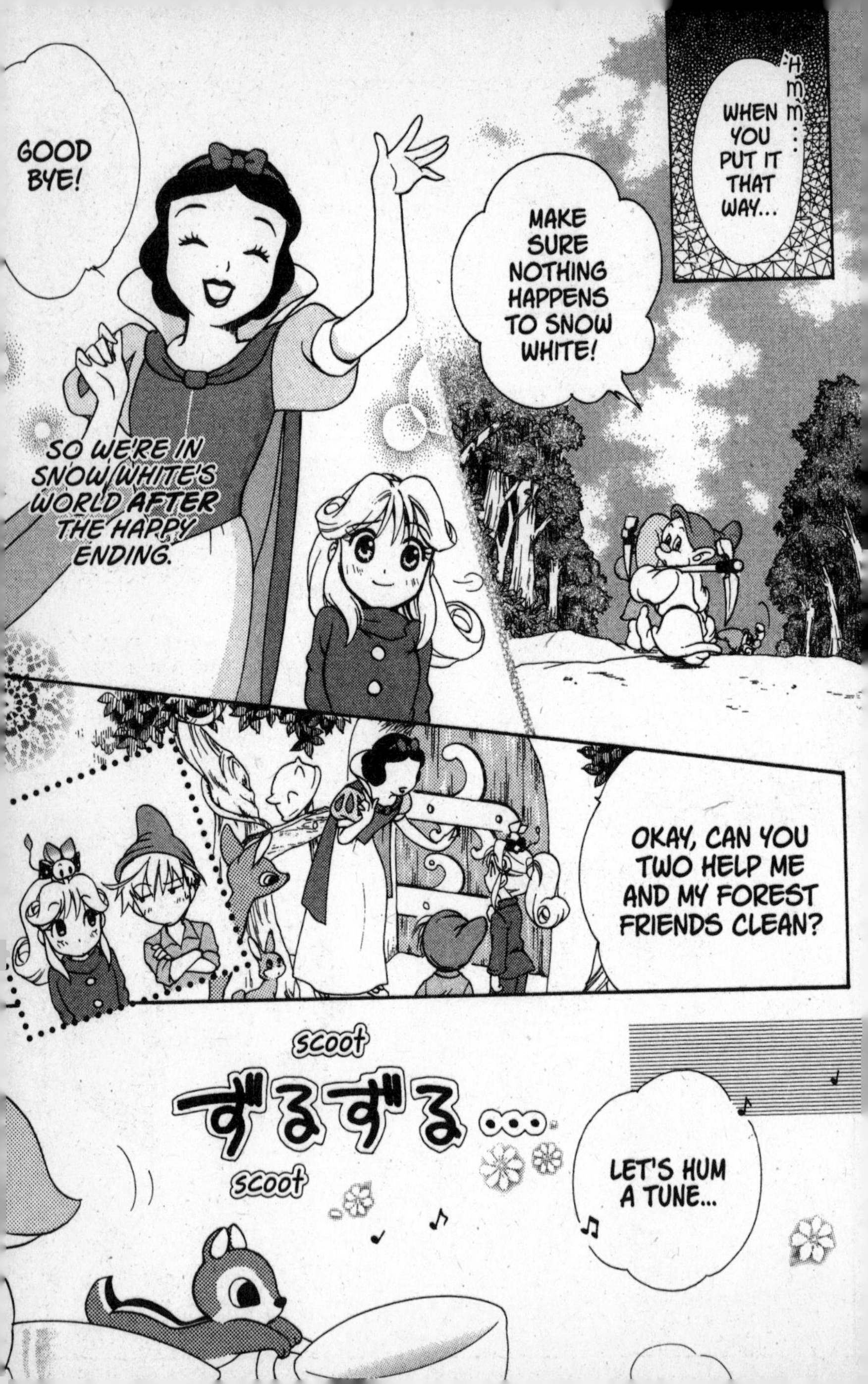
Hmm...
WHEN YOU PUT IT THAT WAY...
MAKE SURE NOTHING HAPPENS TO SNOW WHITE!
GOOD BYE!
SO WE'RE IN SNOW WHITE'S WORLD AFTER THE HAPPY ENDING.
OKAY, CAN YOU TWO HELP ME AND MY FOREST FRIENDS CLEAN?
LET'S HUM A TUNE...
ずるずる...
scoot
scoot

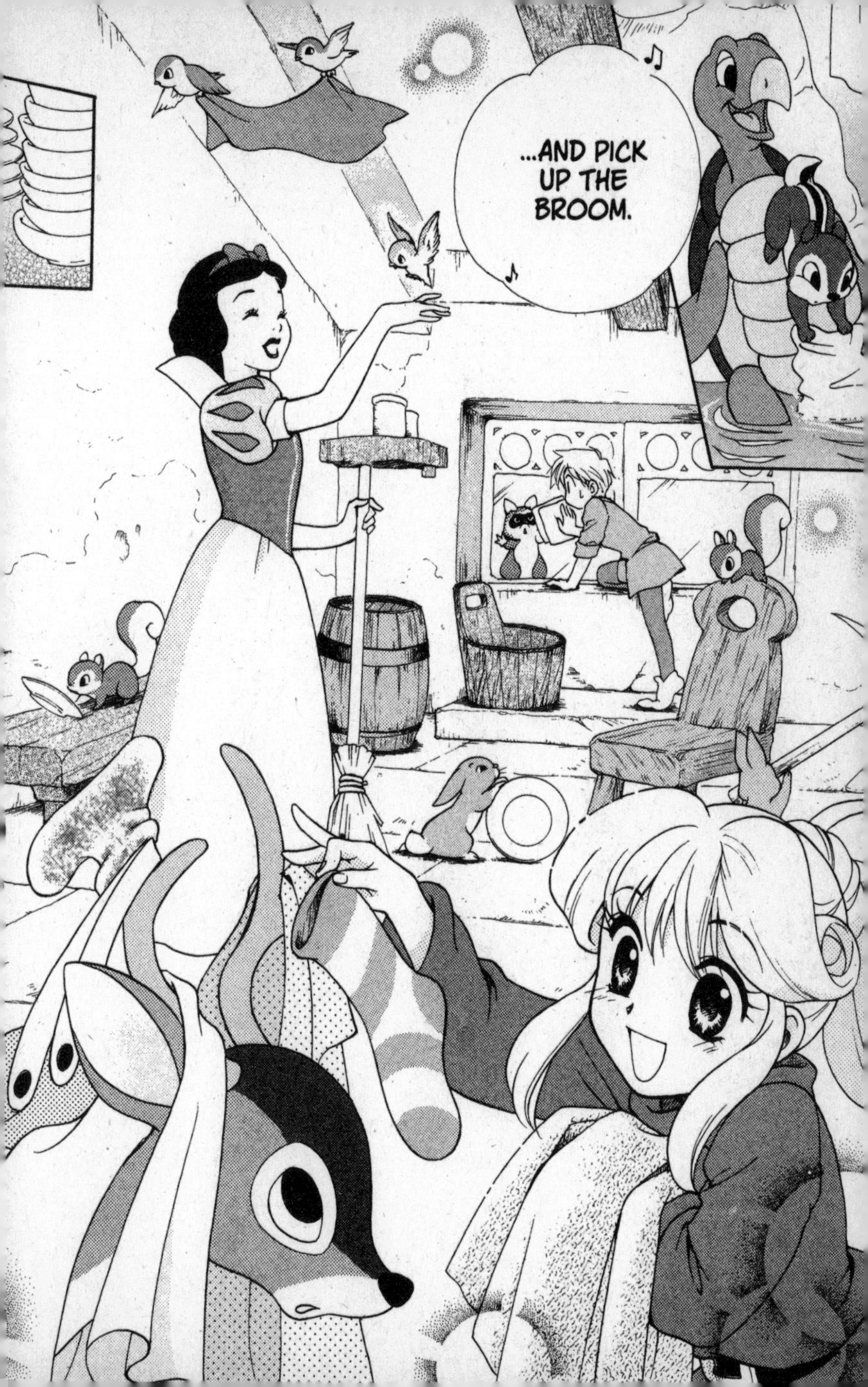
...AND PICK UP THE BROOM.

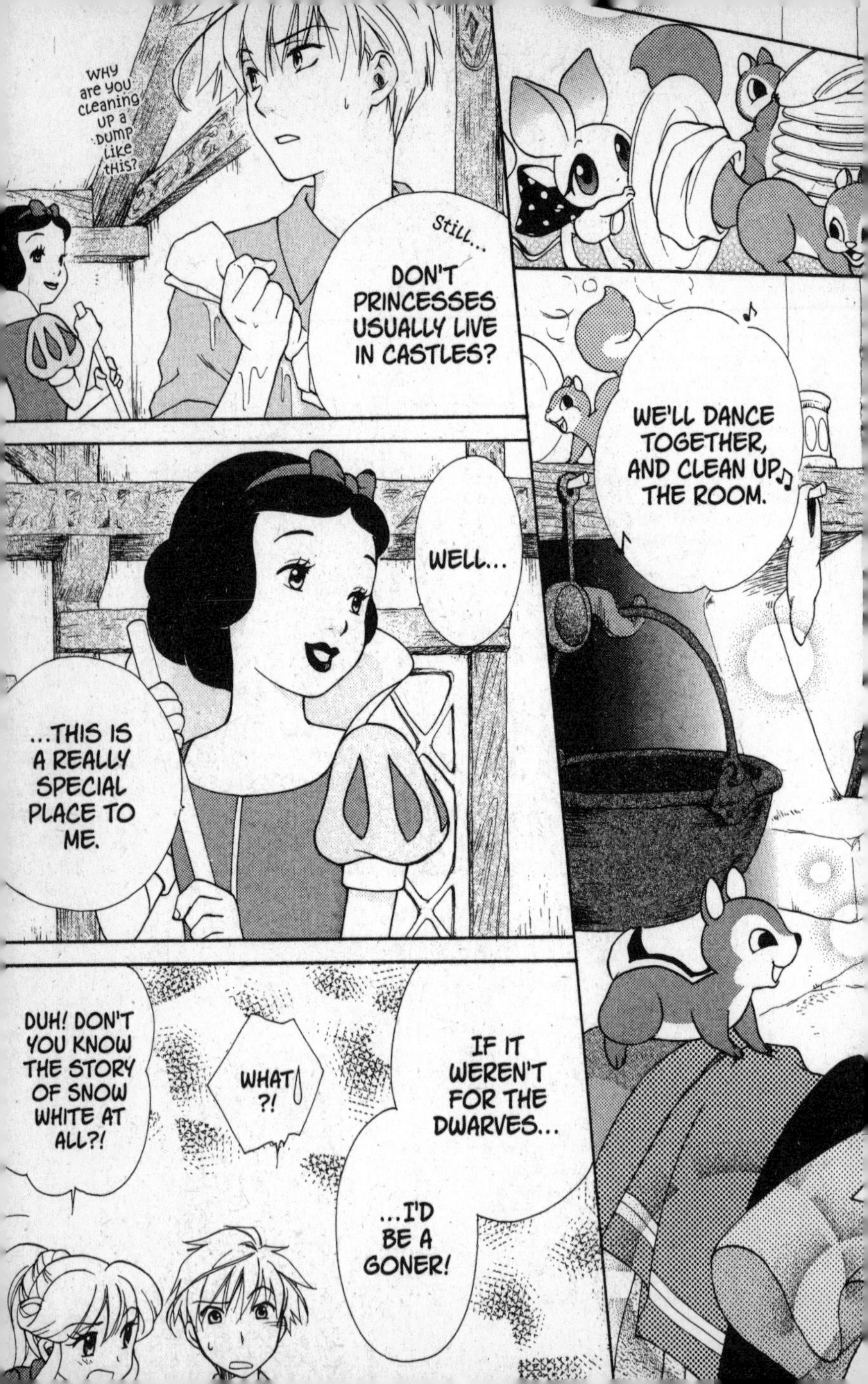
WHY are you cleaning up a DUMP like tHIS?
Still...
DON'T PRINCESSES USUALLY LIVE IN CASTLES?
WE'LL DANCE TOGETHER, AND CLEAN UP THE ROOM.
WELL...
...THIS IS A REALLY SPECIAL PLACE TO ME.
IF IT WEREN'T FOR THE DWARVES...
...I'D BE A GONER!
WHAT?!
DUH! DON'T YOU KNOW THE STORY OF SNOW WHITE AT ALL?!

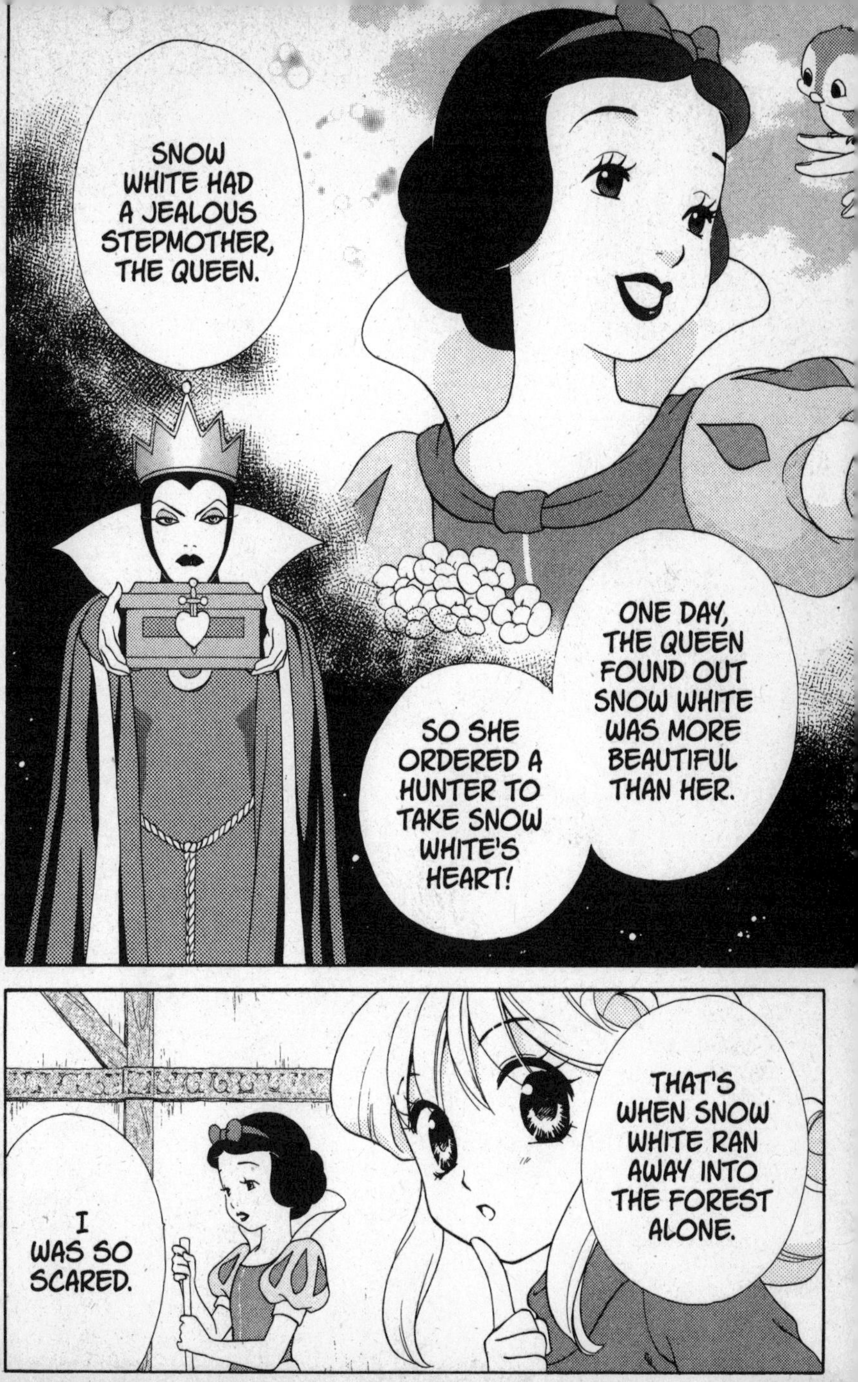
SNOW WHITE HAD A JEALOUS STEPMOTHER, THE QUEEN.
ONE DAY, THE QUEEN FOUND OUT SNOW WHITE WAS MORE BEAUTIFUL THAN HER.
SO SHE ORDERED A HUNTER TO TAKE SNOW WHITE'S HEART!
THAT'S WHEN SNOW WHITE RAN AWAY INTO THE FOREST ALONE.
I WAS SO SCARED.

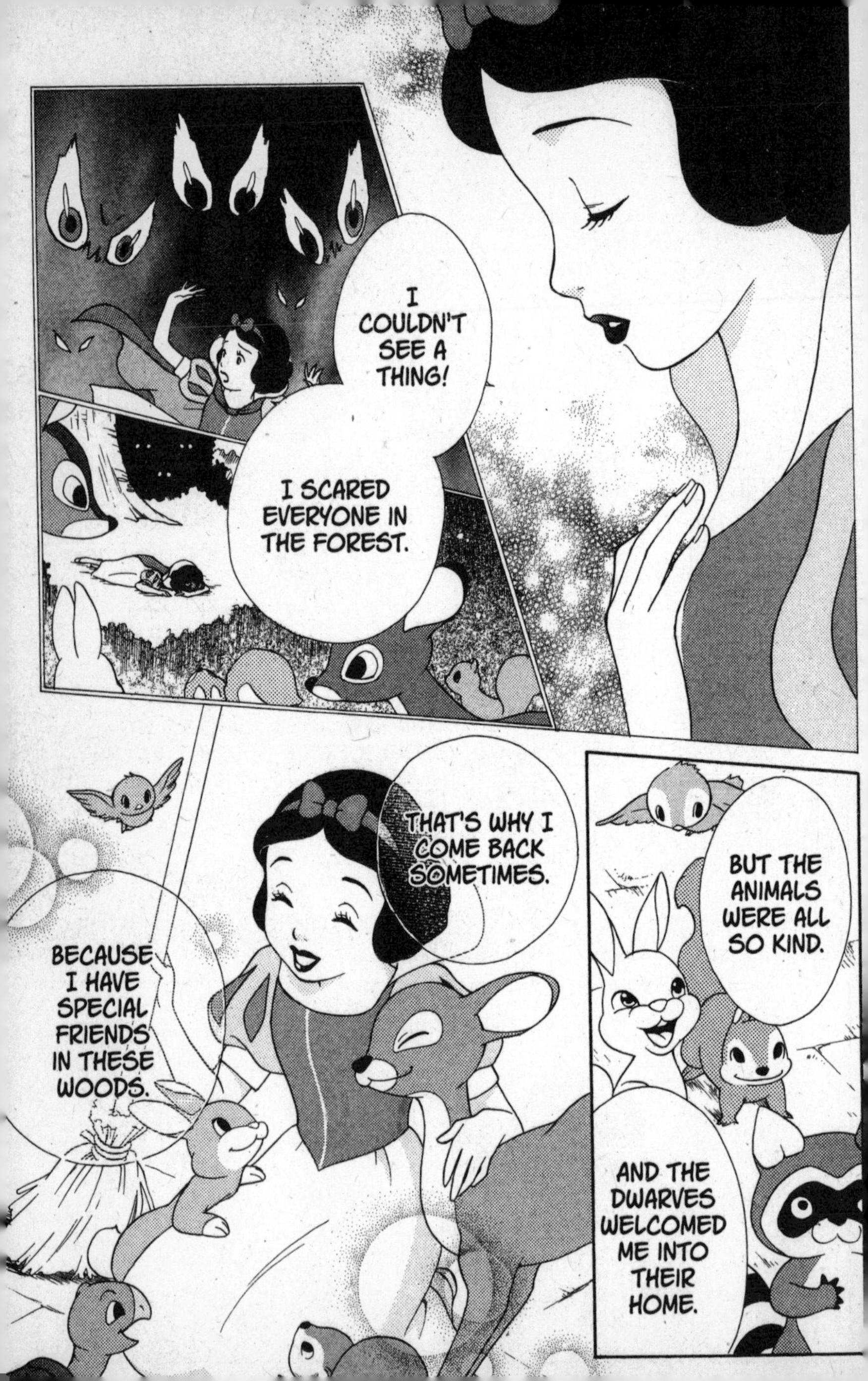
I COULDN'T SEE A THING!
I SCARED EVERYONE IN THE FOREST.
BUT THE ANIMALS WERE ALL SO KIND.
AND THE DWARVES WELCOMED ME INTO THEIR HOME.
THAT'S WHY I COME BACK SOMETIMES.
BECAUSE I HAVE SPECIAL FRIENDS IN THESE WOODS.

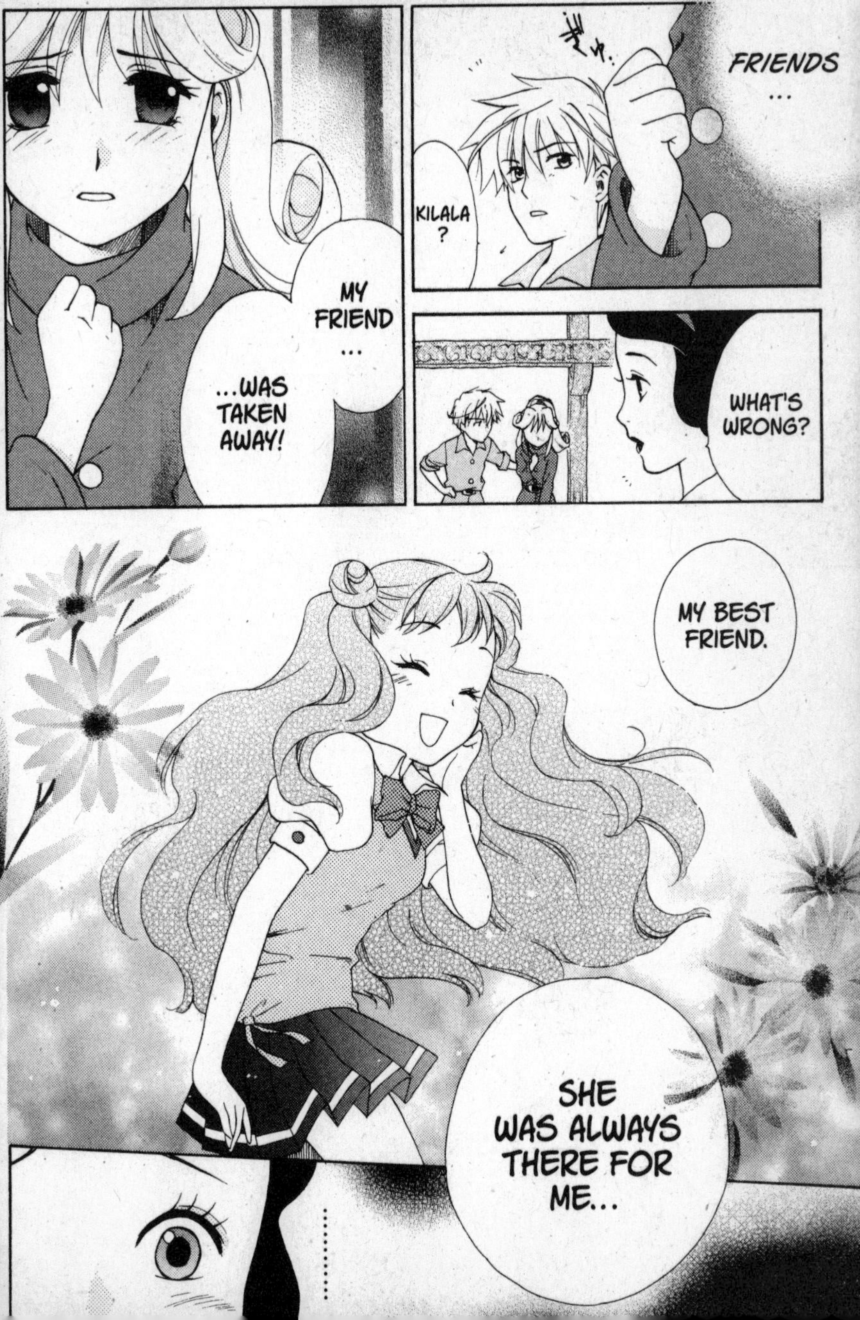
FRIENDS ...
ぎゅ…
KILALA ?
WHAT'S WRONG?
MY FRIEND ...
...WAS TAKEN AWAY!
MY BEST FRIEND.
SHE WAS ALWAYS THERE FOR ME...
......

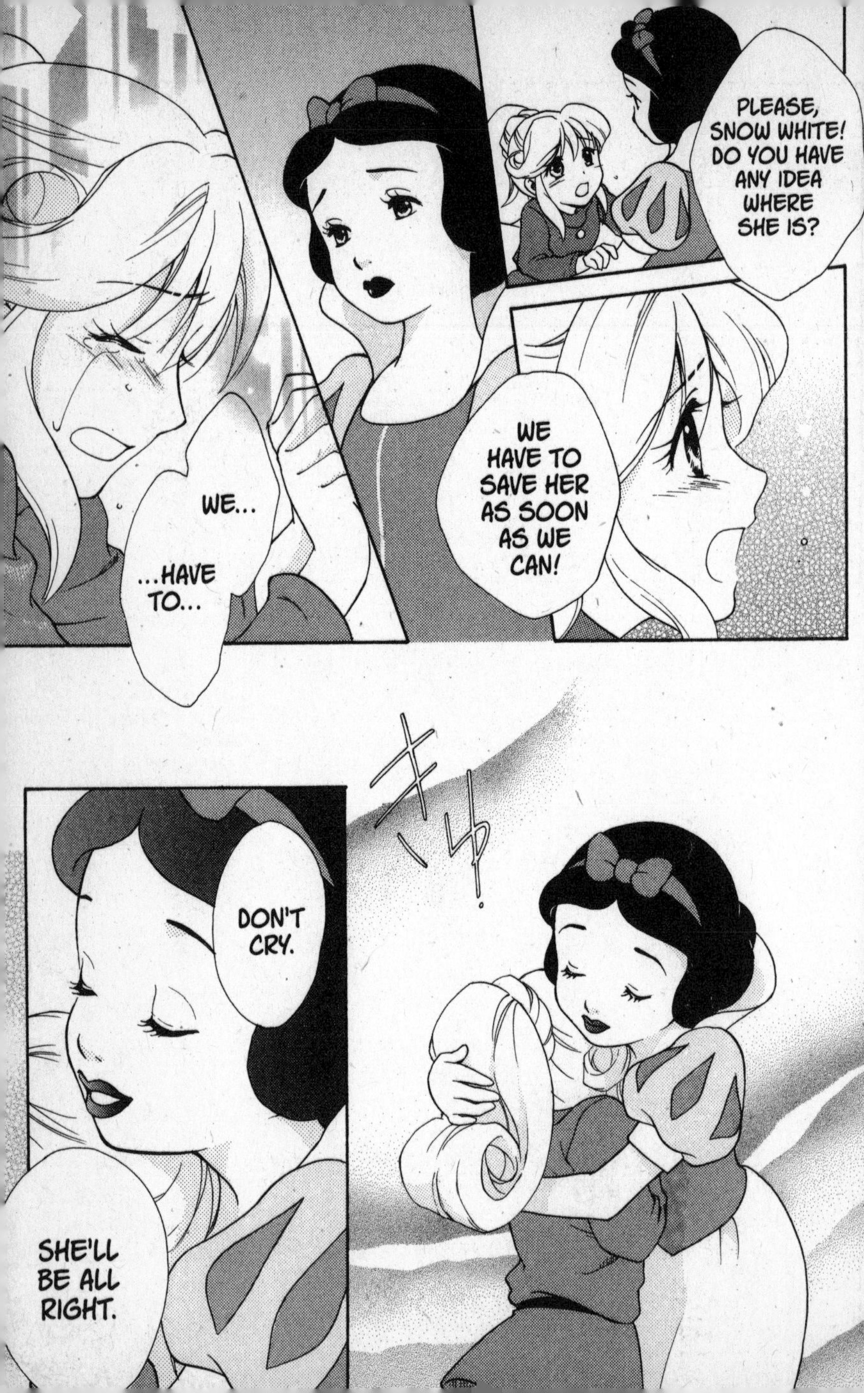
PLEASE, SNOW WHITE! DO YOU HAVE ANY IDEA WHERE SHE IS?
WE HAVE TO SAVE HER AS SOON AS WE CAN!
WE...
...HAVE TO...
DON'T CRY.
SHE'LL BE ALL RIGHT.

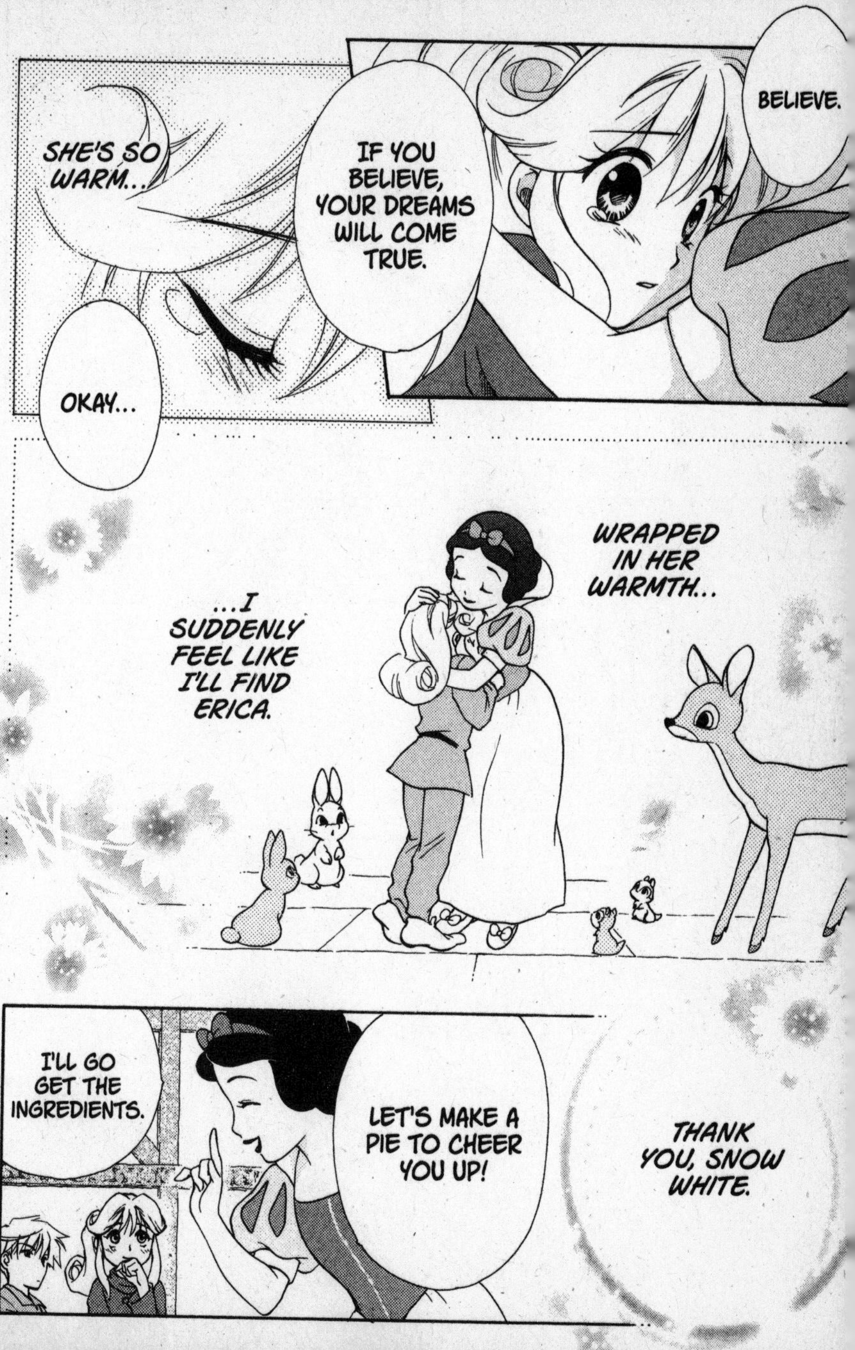
BELIEVE.
IF YOU BELIEVE, YOUR DREAMS WILL COME TRUE.
SHE'S SO WARM...
OKAY...
WRAPPED IN HER WARMTH...
...I SUDDENLY FEEL LIKE I'LL FIND ERICA.
THANK YOU, SNOW WHITE.
LET'S MAKE A PIE TO CHEER YOU UP!
I'LL GO GET THE INGREDIENTS.

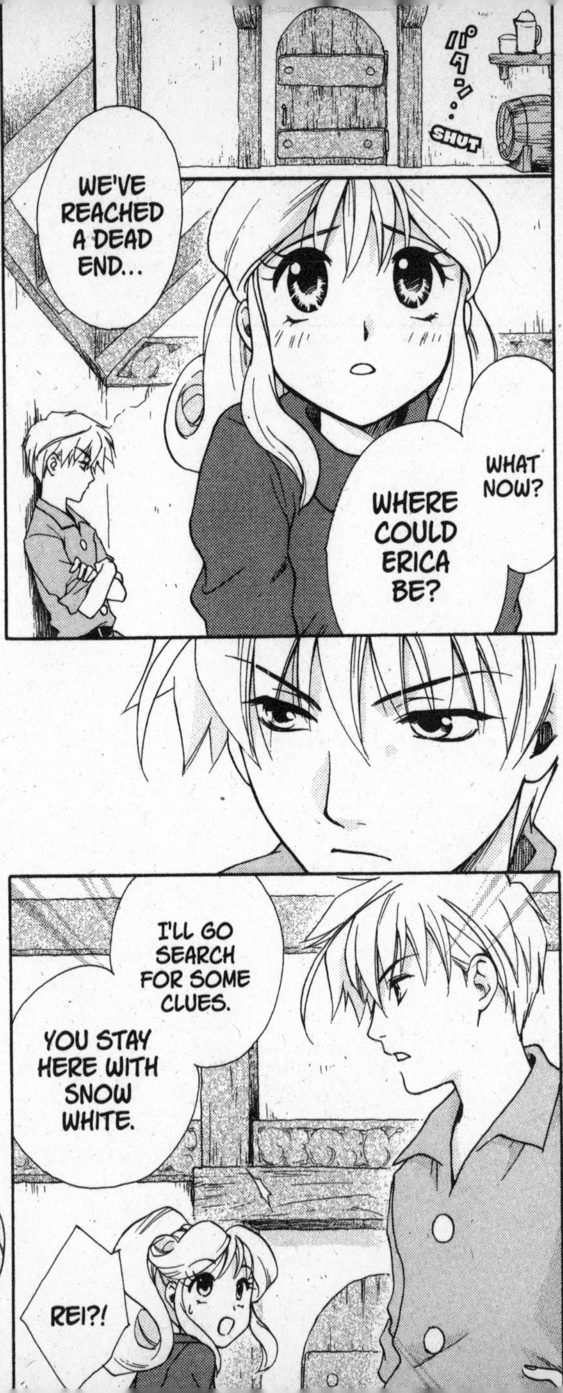
SHUT
WE'VE REACHED A DEAD END...
WHAT NOW?
WHERE COULD ERICA BE?
I'LL GO SEARCH FOR SOME CLUES.
YOU STAY HERE WITH SNOW WHITE.
REI?!

Ariel

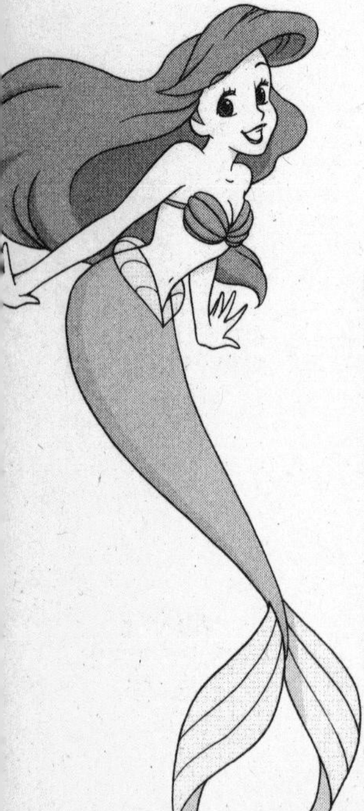

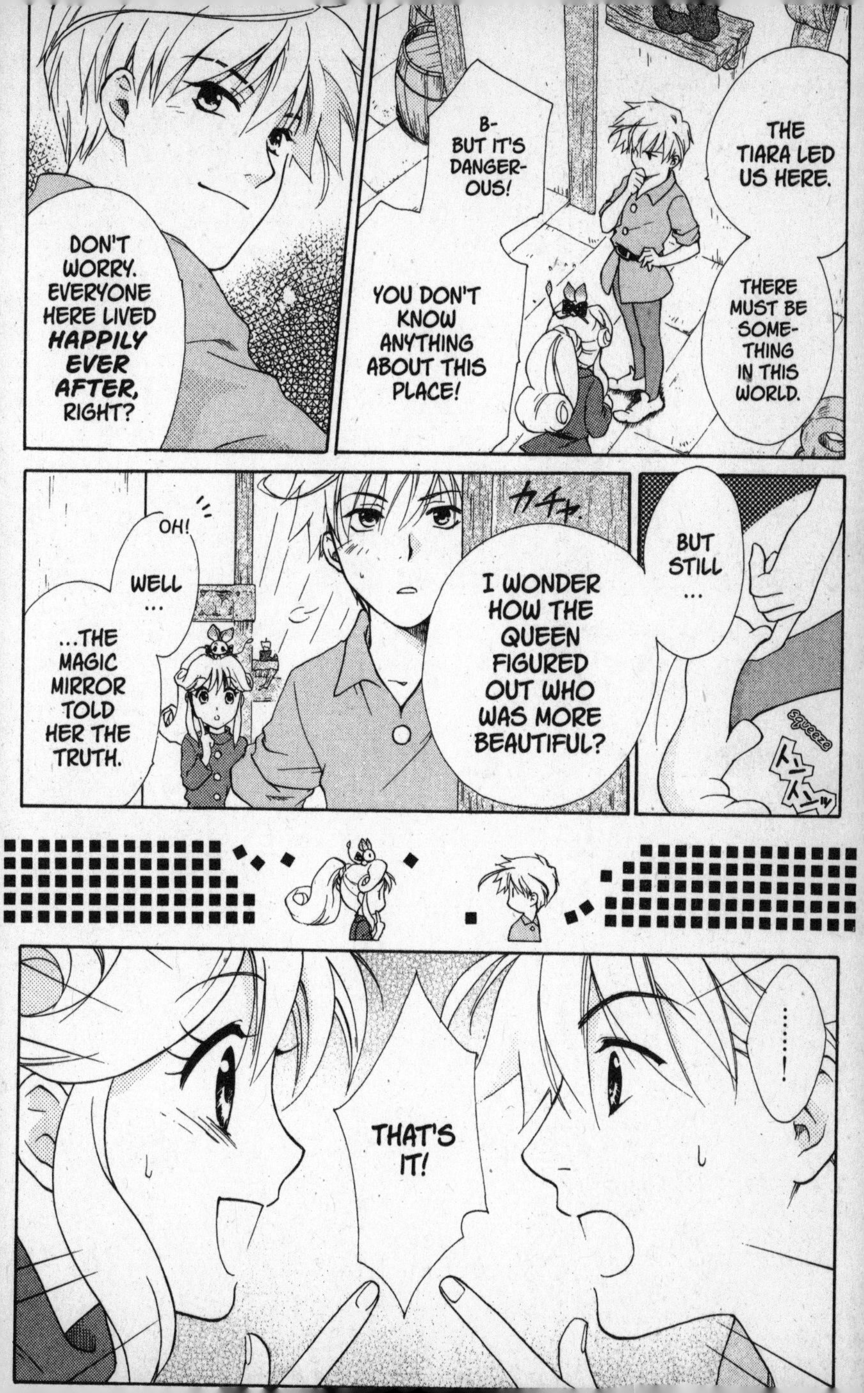
THE TIARA LED US HERE.
THERE MUST BE SOME-THING IN THIS WORLD.
B- BUT IT'S DANGER-OUS!
YOU DON'T KNOW ANYTHING ABOUT THIS PLACE!
DON'T WORRY. EVERYONE HERE LIVED *HAPPILY EVER AFTER*, RIGHT?
BUT STILL ...
squeeze
カチャ
I WONDER HOW THE QUEEN FIGURED OUT WHO WAS MORE BEAUTIFUL?
OH!
WELL ...
...THE MAGIC MIRROR TOLD HER THE TRUTH.
......!
THAT'S IT!

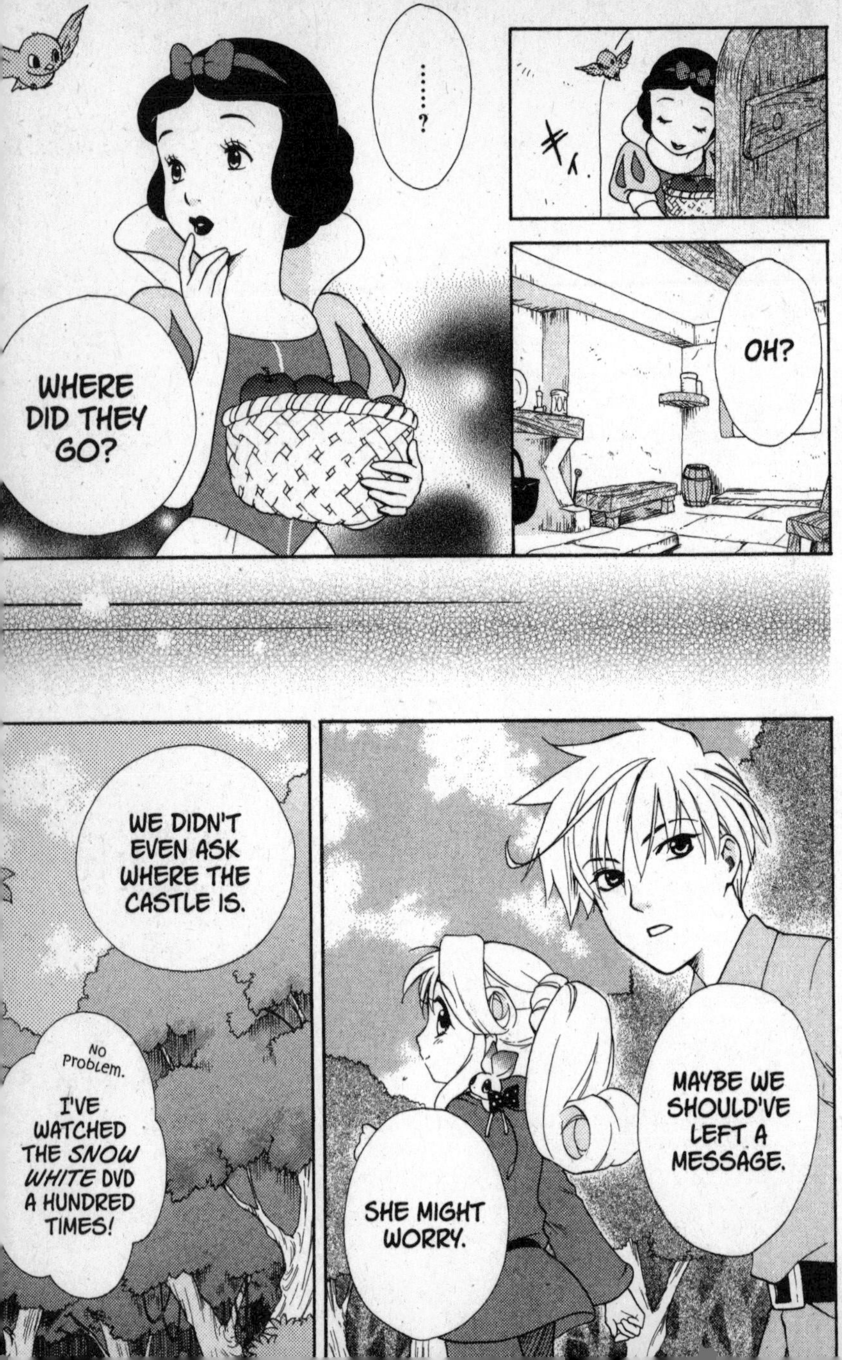
キィ
OH?
......?
WHERE DID THEY GO?
MAYBE WE SHOULD'VE LEFT A MESSAGE.
SHE MIGHT WORRY.
WE DIDN'T EVEN ASK WHERE THE CASTLE IS.
No problem.
I'VE WATCHED THE *SNOW WHITE* DVD A HUNDRED TIMES!

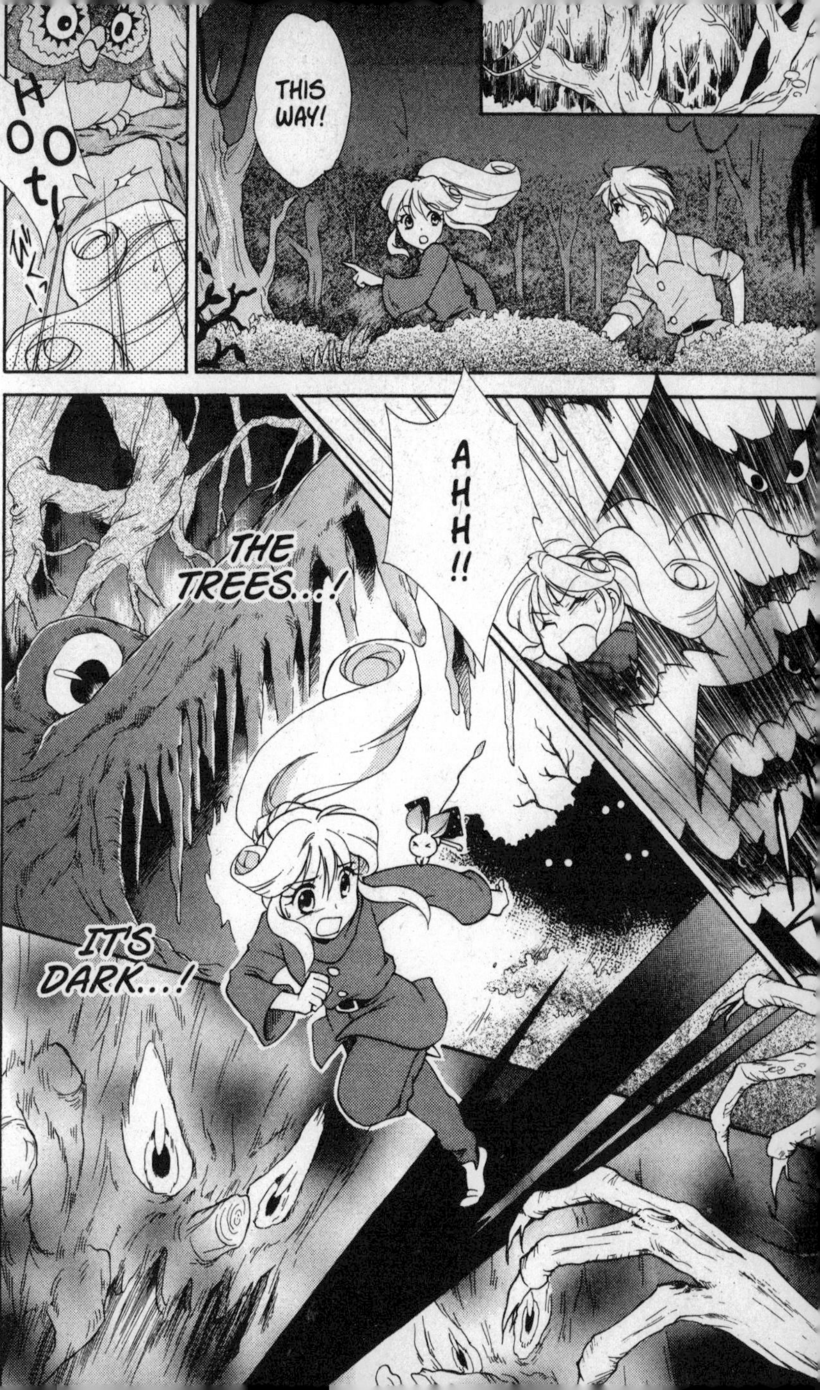
THIS WAY!
HOOt!
びくっ!
AHHH!!
THE TREES...!
IT'S DARK...!

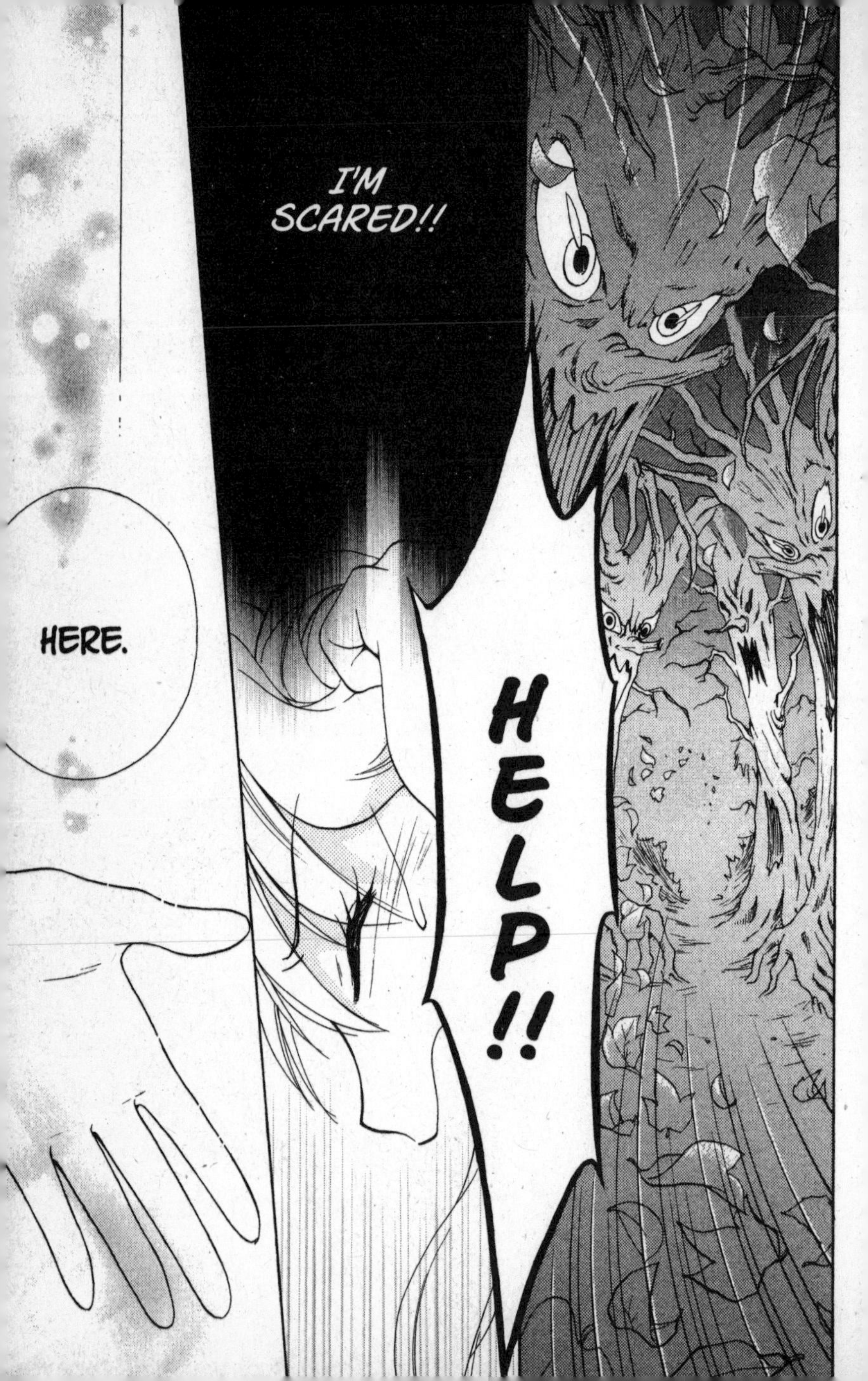
I'M SCARED!!
HELP!!
HERE.

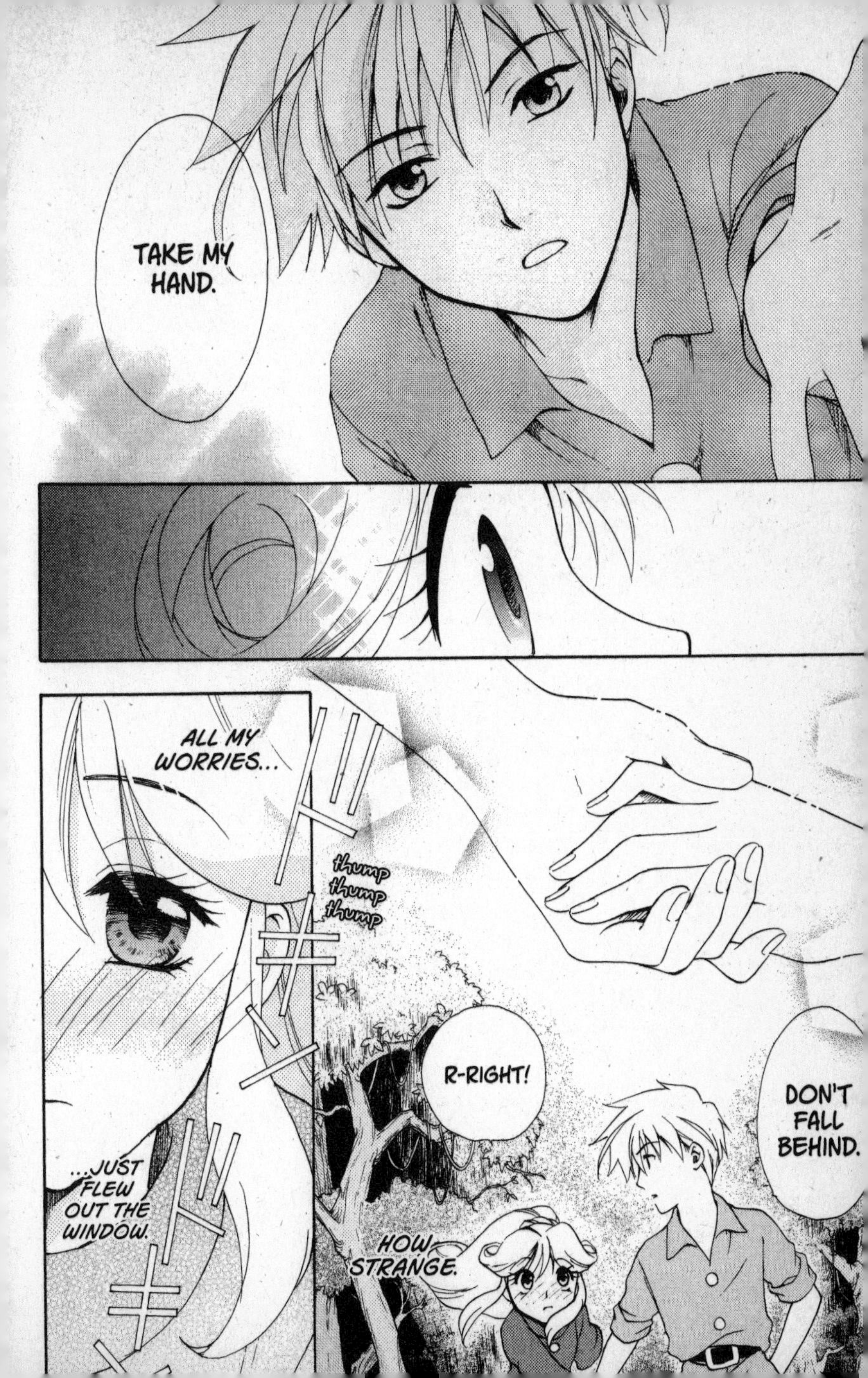
TAKE MY HAND.
DON'T FALL BEHIND.
R-RIGHT!
HOW STRANGE.
ALL MY WORRIES...
thump thump thump
...JUST FLEW OUT THE WINDOW.

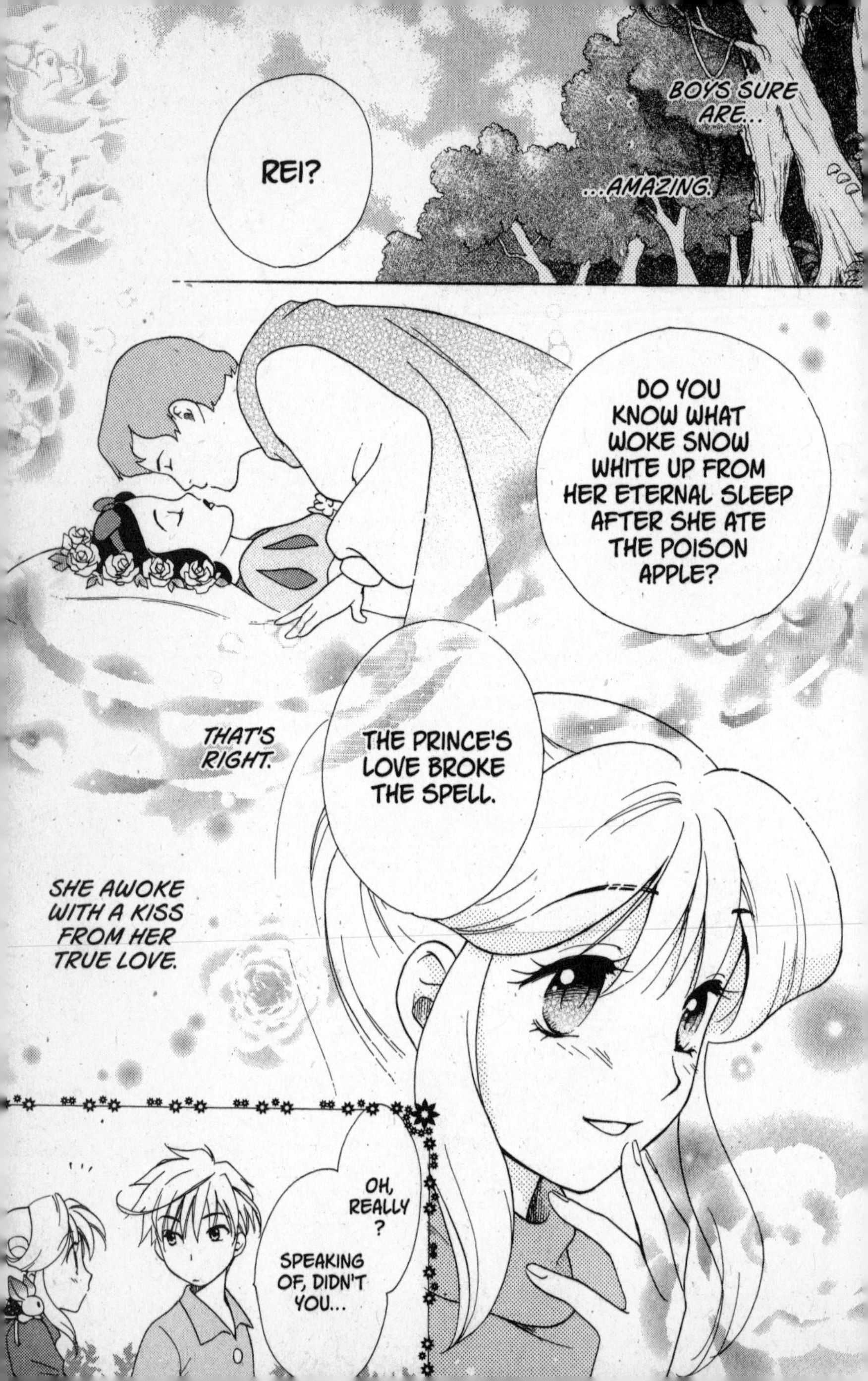
BOYS SURE ARE...
...AMAZING.
REI?
DO YOU KNOW WHAT WOKE SNOW WHITE UP FROM HER ETERNAL SLEEP AFTER SHE ATE THE POISON APPLE?
THE PRINCE'S LOVE BROKE THE SPELL.
THAT'S RIGHT.
SHE AWOKE WITH A KISS FROM HER TRUE LOVE.
OH, REALLY?
SPEAKING OF, DIDN'T YOU...

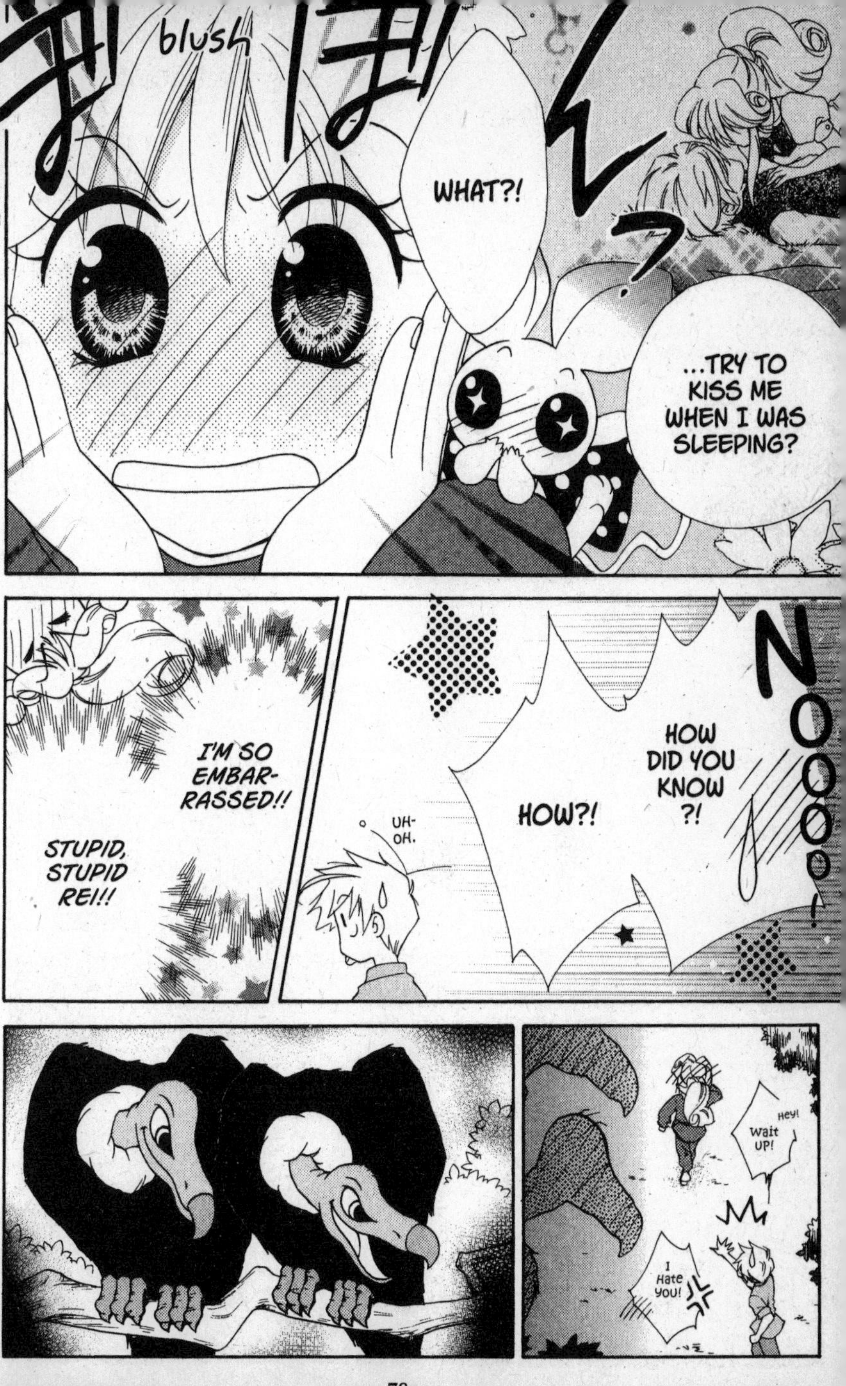
...TRY TO KISS ME WHEN I WAS SLEEPING?
WHAT?!
blush
NOOOO!
HOW DID YOU KNOW?!
HOW?!
UH-OH.
I'M SO EMBARRASSED!!
STUPID, STUPID REI!!
Hey! Wait UP!
I Hate you!

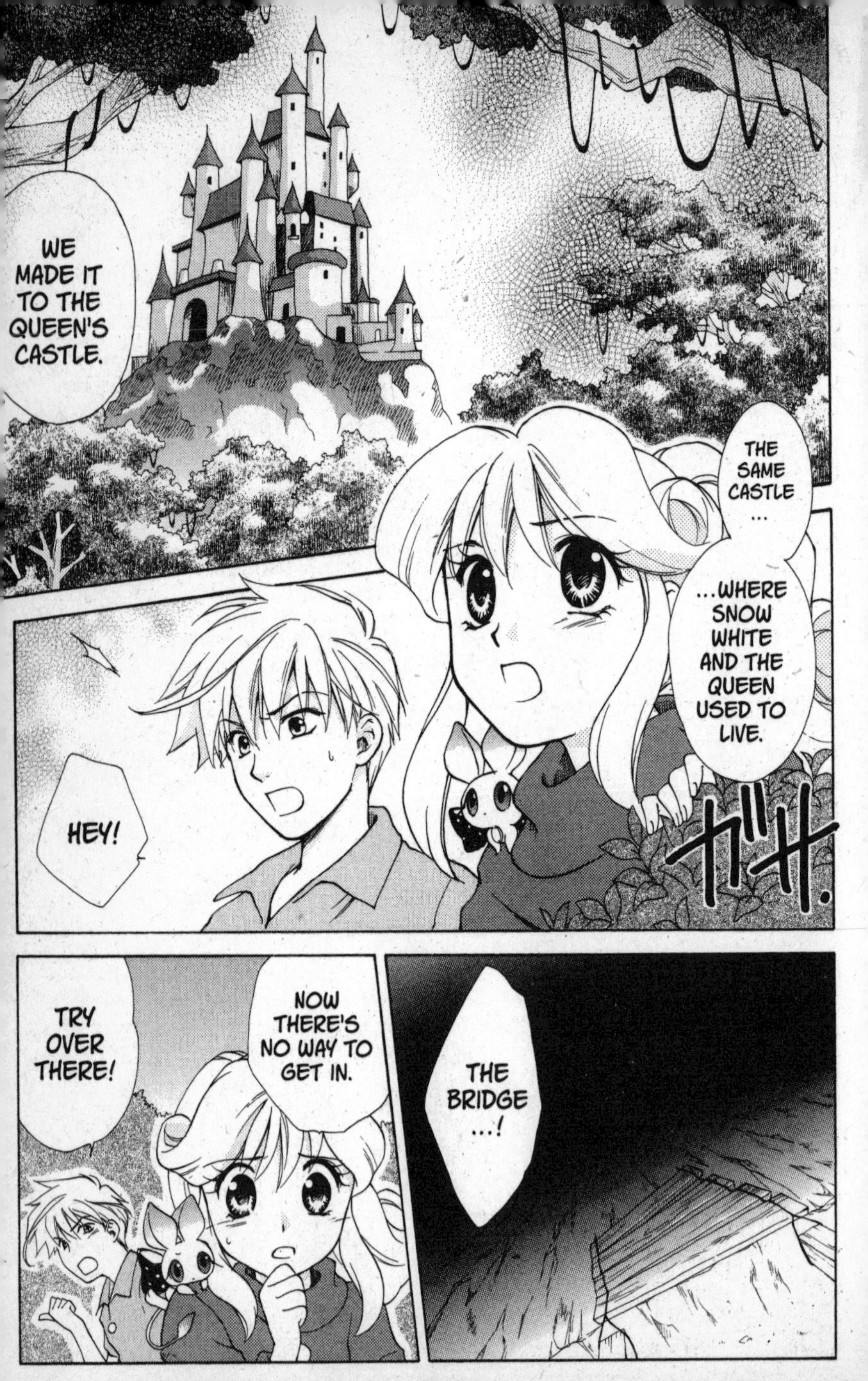
WE MADE IT TO THE QUEEN'S CASTLE.
THE SAME CASTLE...
...WHERE SNOW WHITE AND THE QUEEN USED TO LIVE.
ガサ.
HEY!
THE BRIDGE...!
NOW THERE'S NO WAY TO GET IN.
TRY OVER THERE!

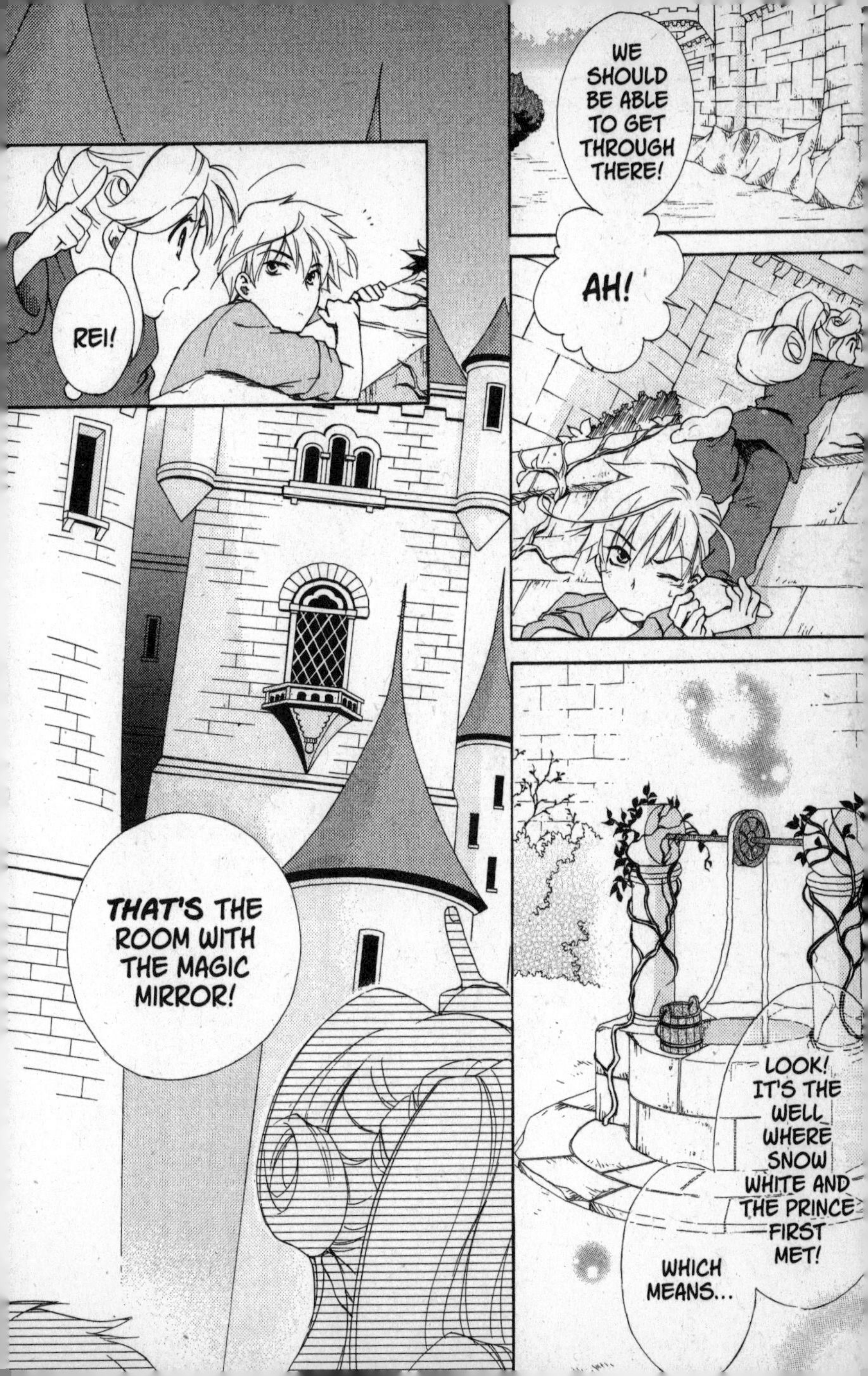
WE SHOULD BE ABLE TO GET THROUGH THERE!
AH!
LOOK! IT'S THE WELL WHERE SNOW WHITE AND THE PRINCE FIRST MET!
WHICH MEANS...
REI!
THAT'S THE ROOM WITH THE MAGIC MIRROR!

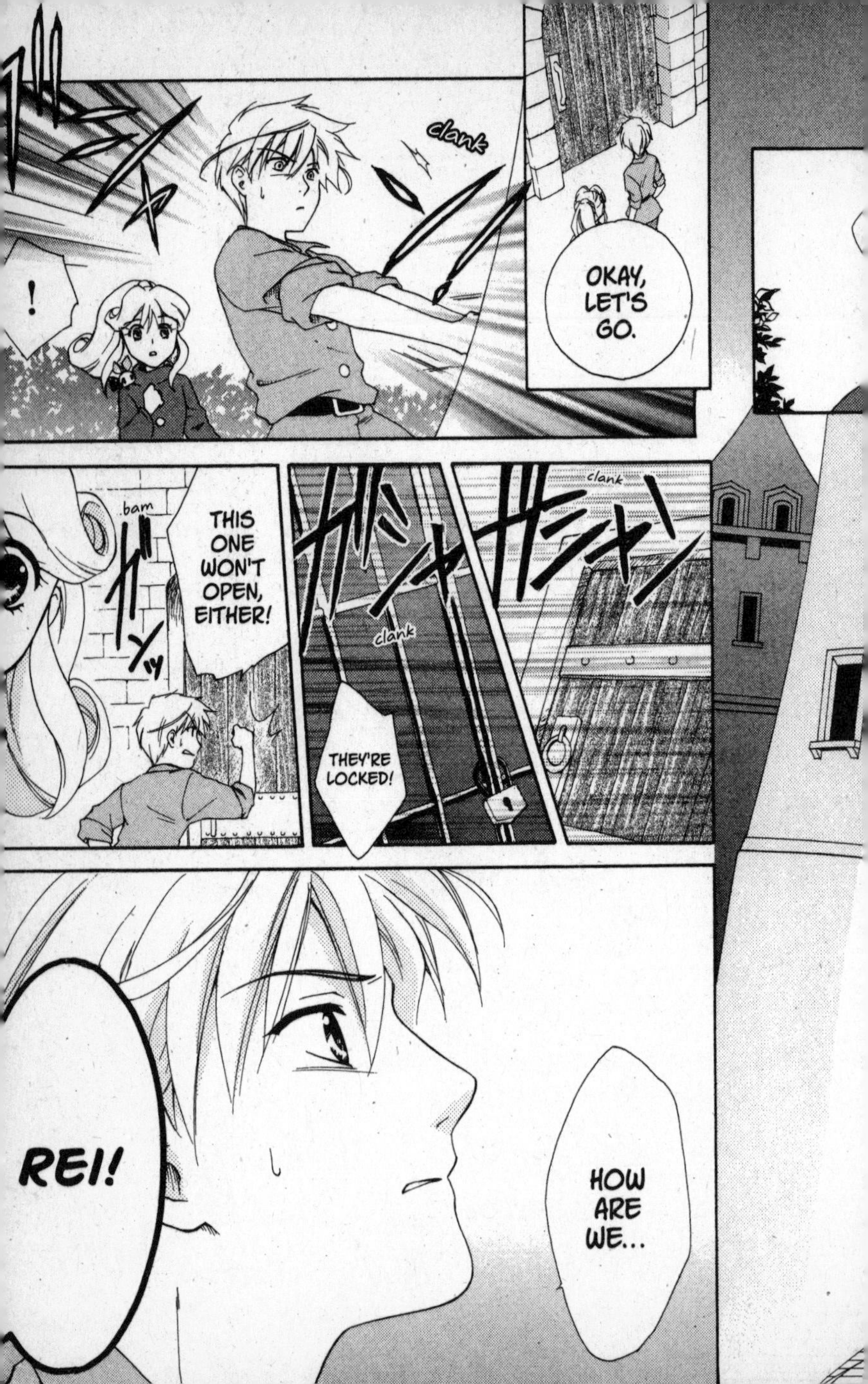
OKAY, LET'S GO.
clank
!
clank
clank
THEY'RE LOCKED!
bam
THIS ONE WON'T OPEN, EITHER!
HOW ARE WE...
REI!

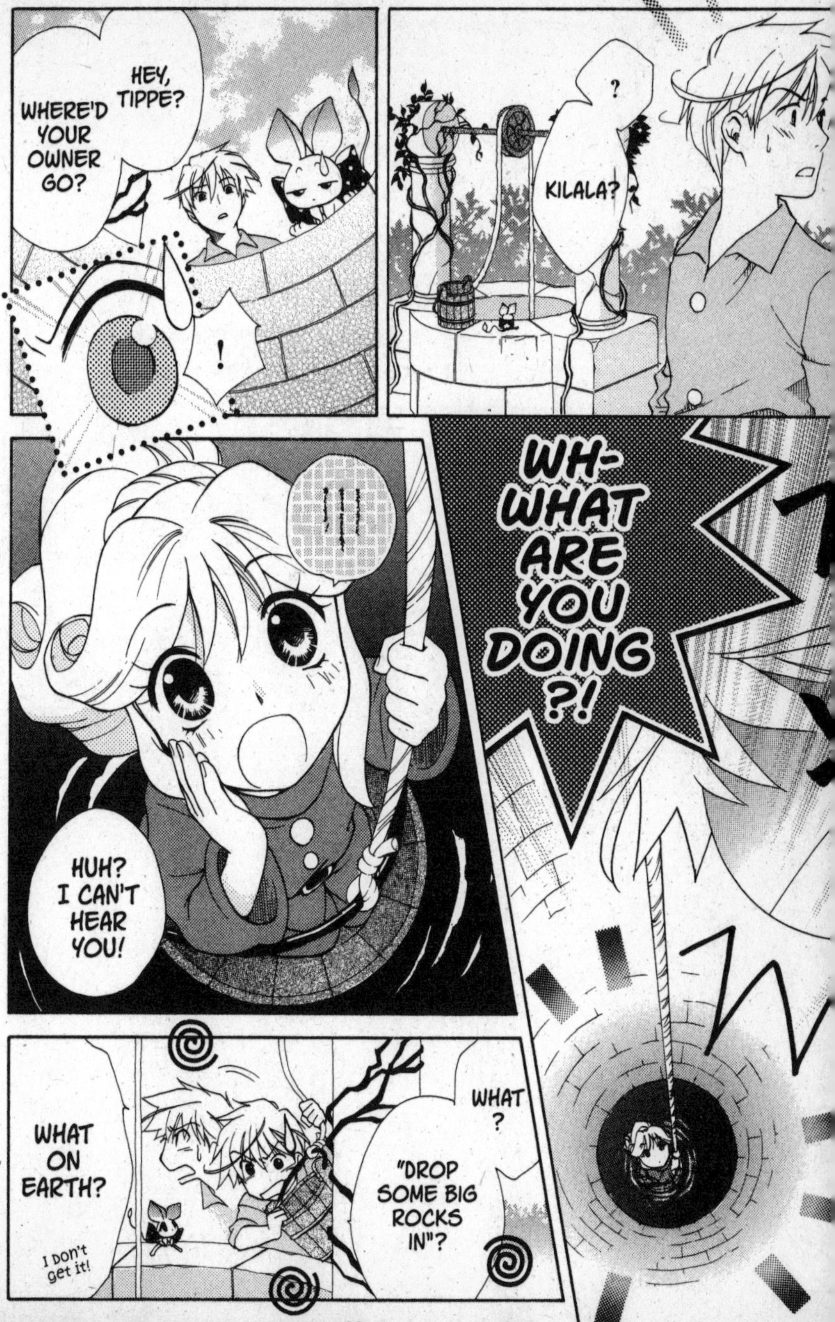
?
KILALA?
HEY, TIPPE? WHERE'D YOUR OWNER GO?
!
WH-WHAT ARE YOU DOING?!
HUH? I CAN'T HEAR YOU!
WHAT?
"DROP SOME BIG ROCKS IN"?
WHAT ON EARTH?
I Don't get it!

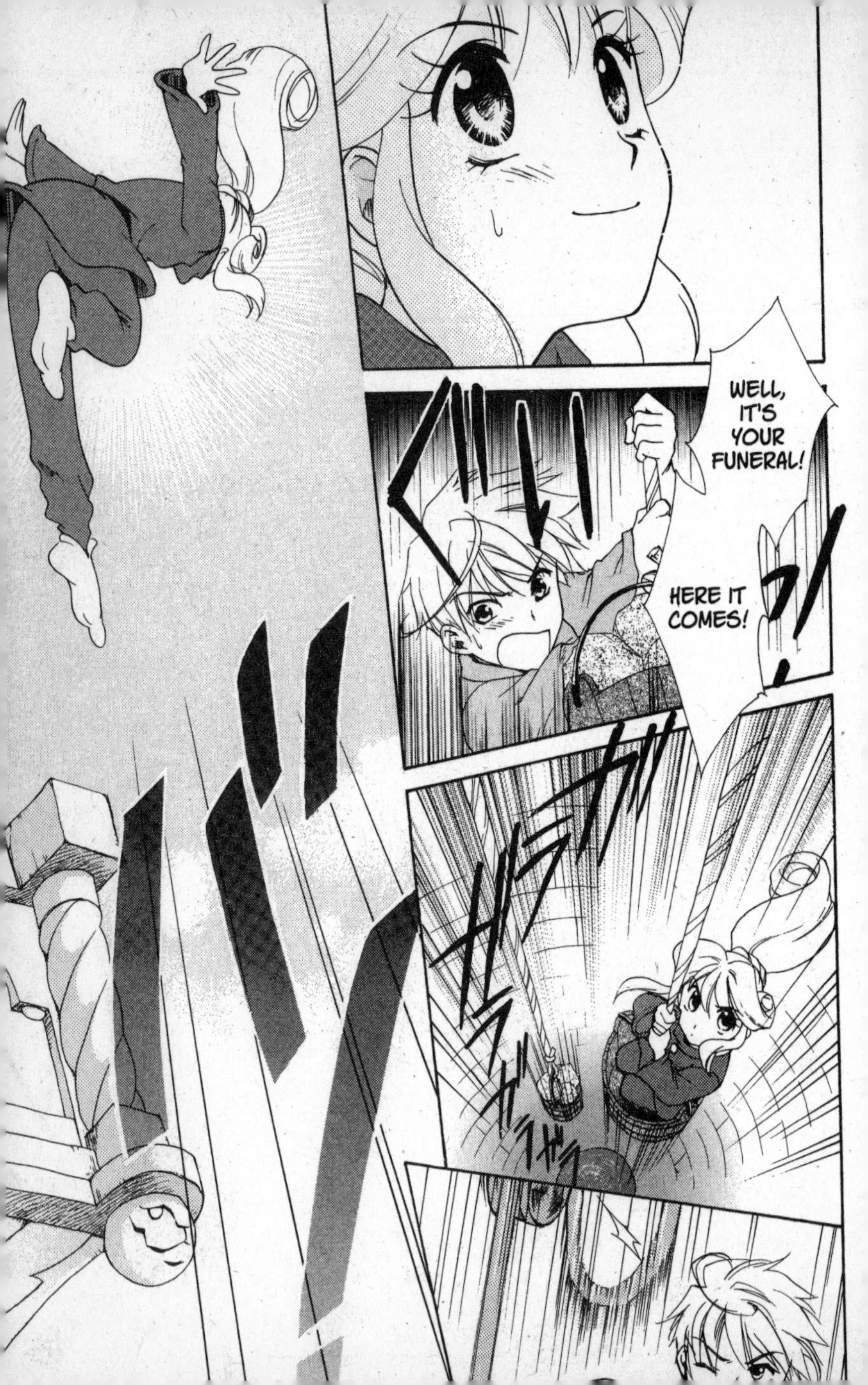
WELL, IT'S YOUR FUNERAL!
HERE IT COMES!

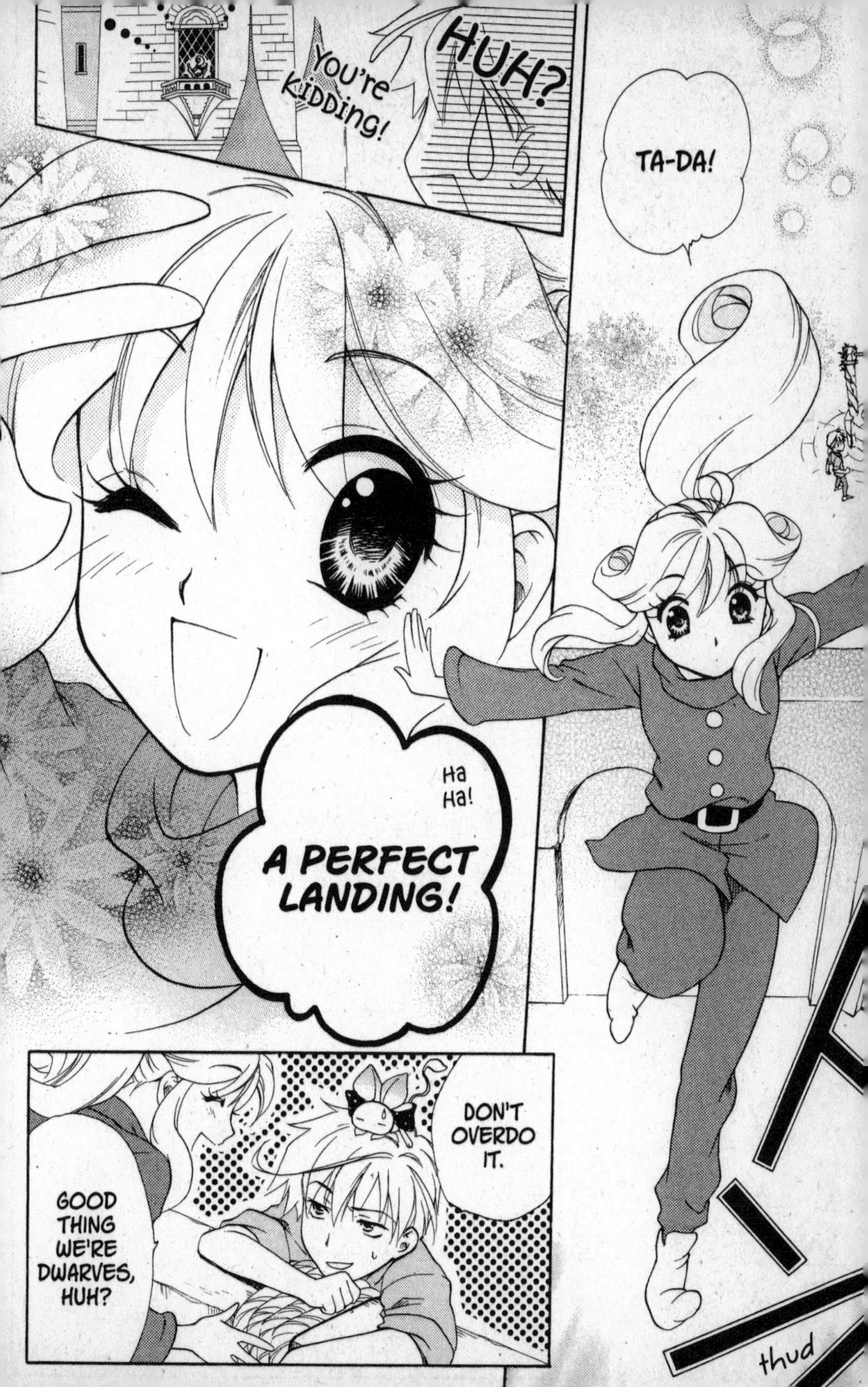
TA-DA!
thud
HUH?
You're kidding!
Ha Ha!
A PERFECT LANDING!
DON'T OVERDO IT.
GOOD THING WE'RE DWARVES, HUH?

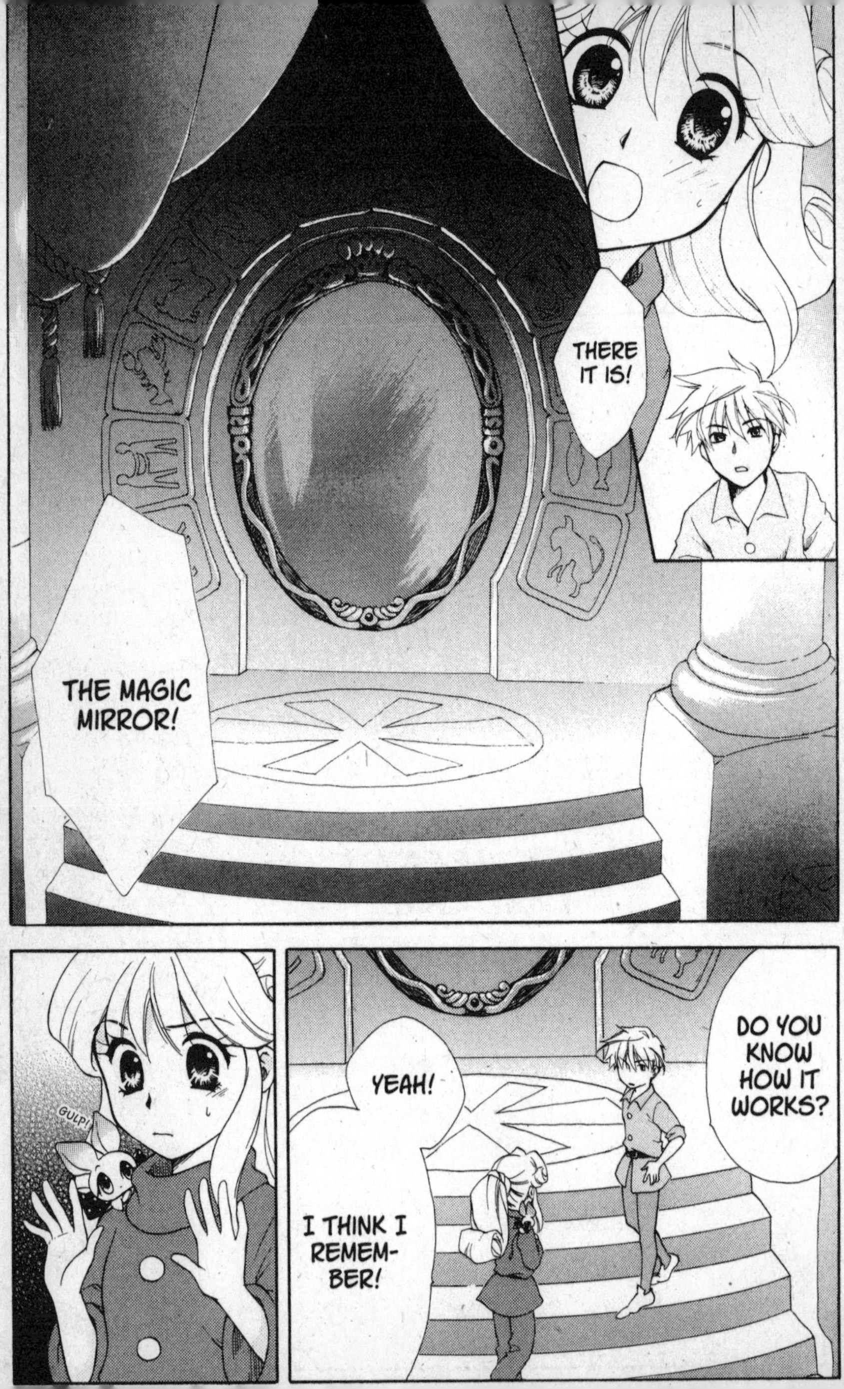
THERE IT IS!
THE MAGIC MIRROR!
DO YOU KNOW HOW IT WORKS?
YEAH!
I THINK I REMEMBER!
GULP!

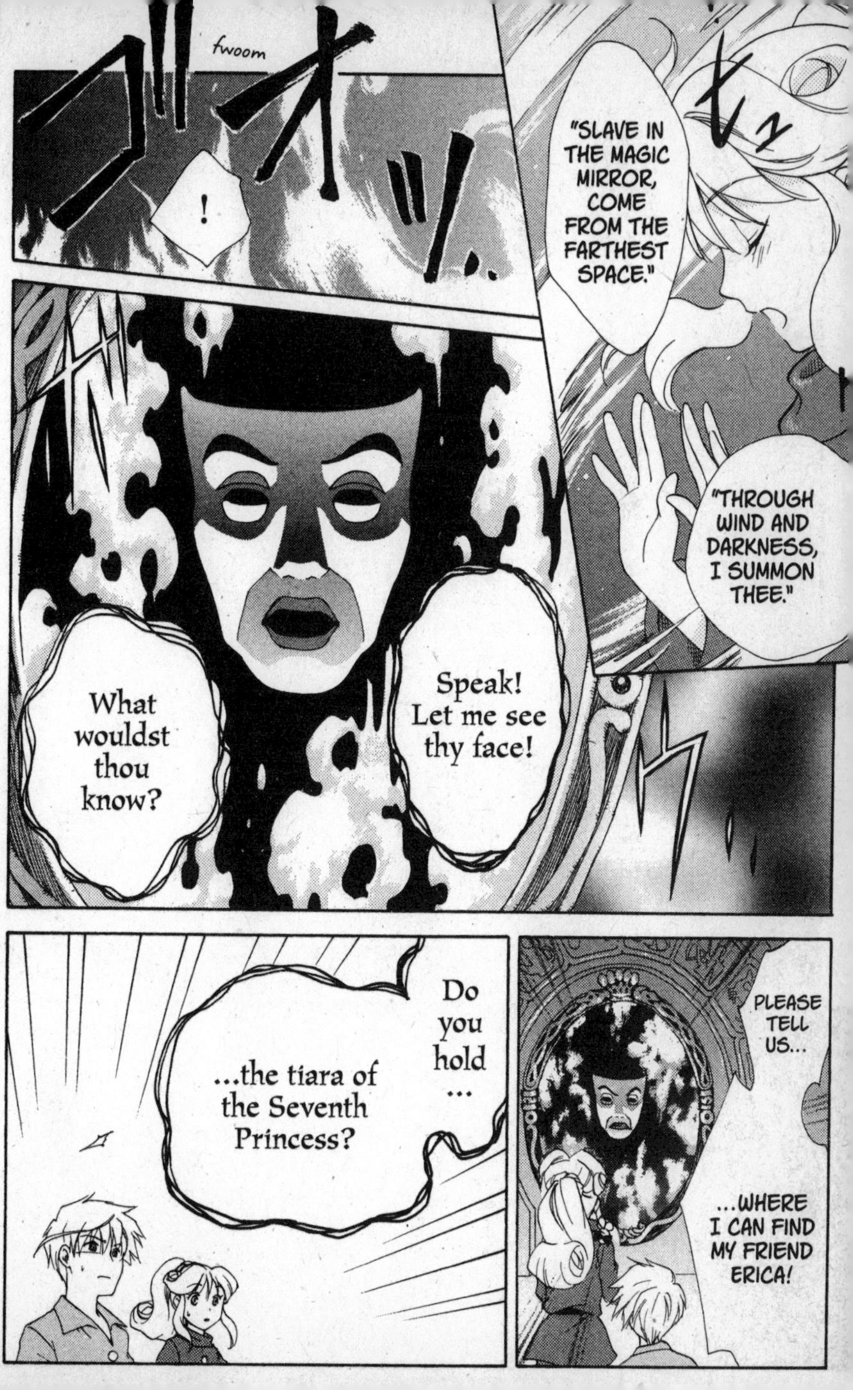
"SLAVE IN THE MAGIC MIRROR, COME FROM THE FARTHEST SPACE."
"THROUGH WIND AND DARKNESS, I SUMMON THEE."
fwoom
!
Speak! Let me see thy face!
What wouldst thou know?
PLEASE TELL US...
...WHERE I CAN FIND MY FRIEND ERICA!
Do you hold ...
...the tiara of the Seventh Princess?

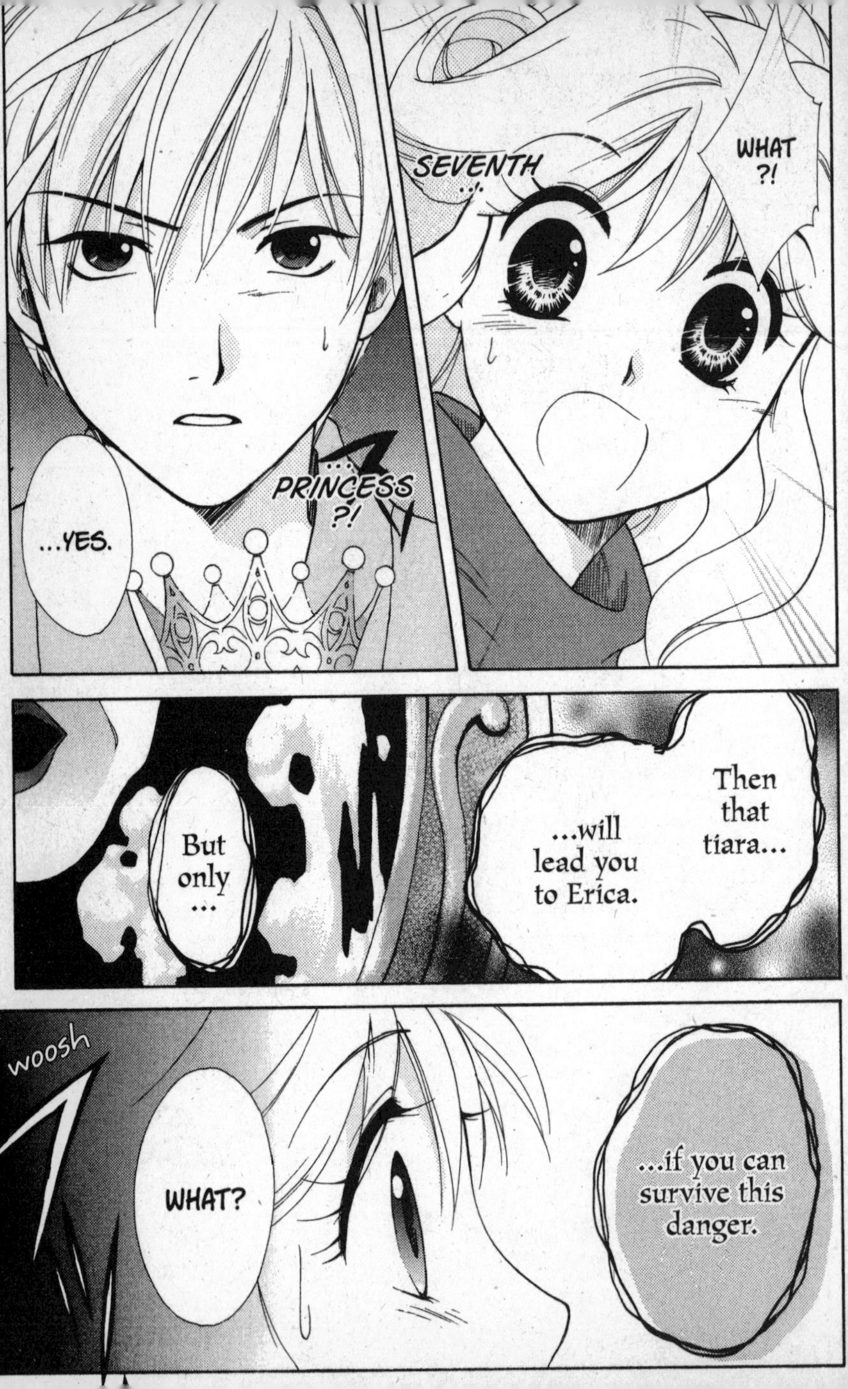
WHAT ?!
SEVENTH ...
...PRINCESS ?!
...YES.
Then that tiara...
...will lead you to Erica.
But only ...
...if you can survive this danger.
WHAT?
woosh

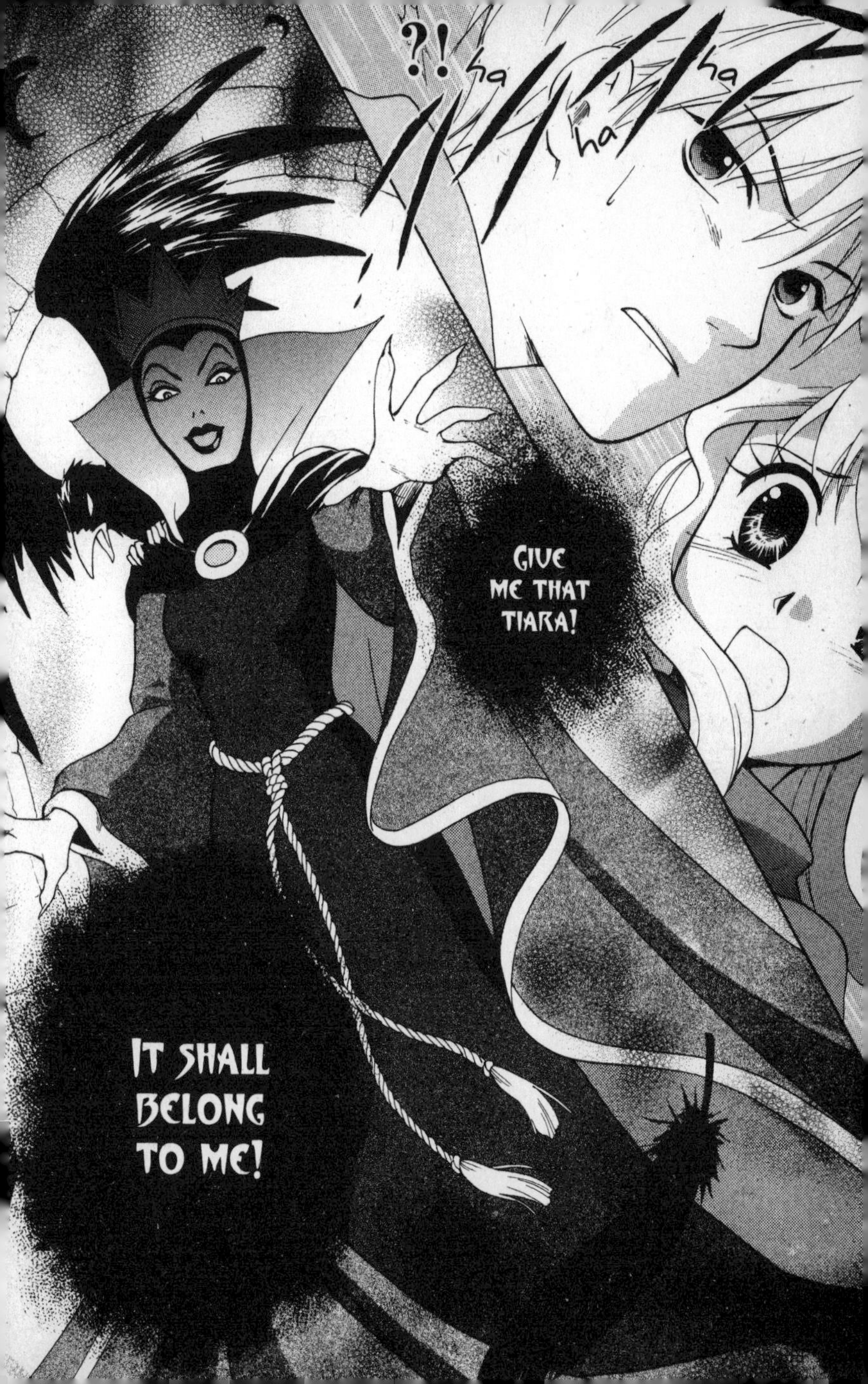
?!
ha
ha
ha
GIVE ME THAT TIARA!
IT SHALL BELONG TO ME!

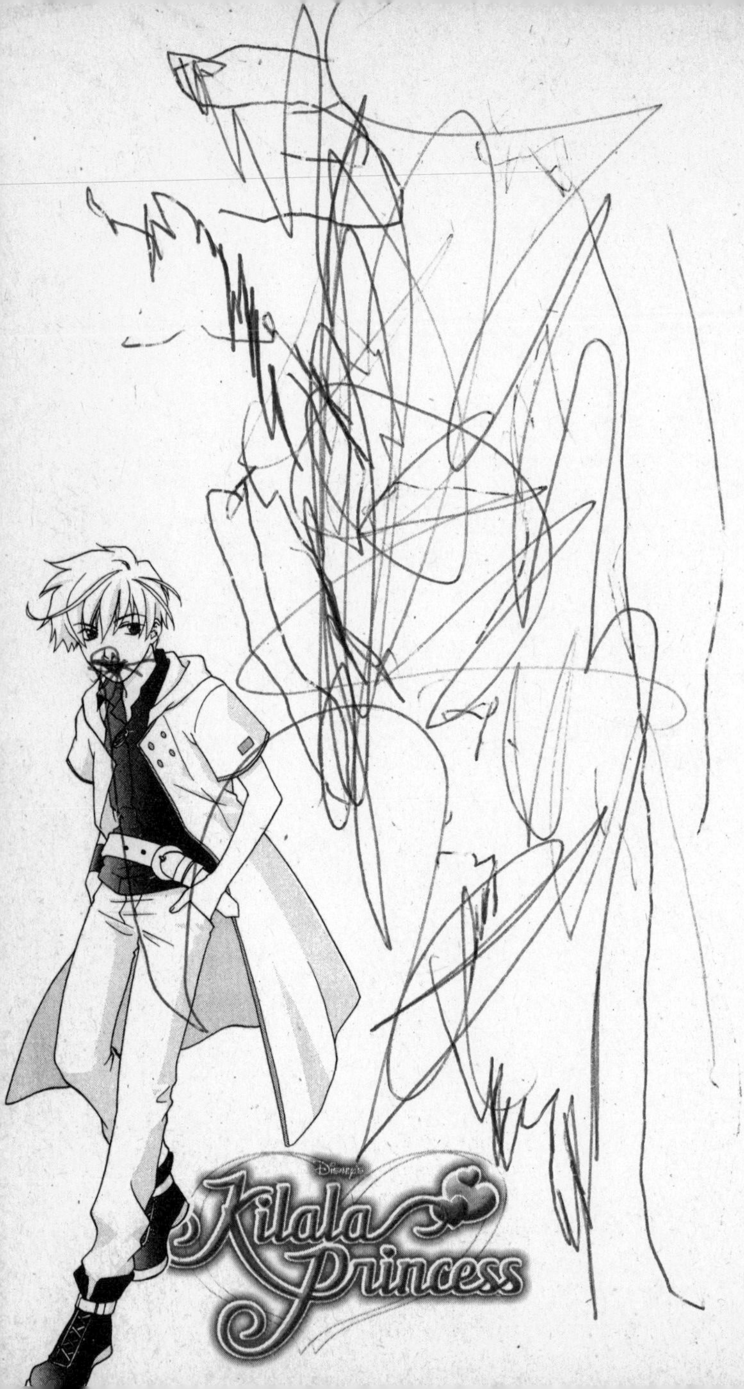
Disney's
Kilala Princess

IN THE NEXT VOLUME OF

DISNEY'S
Kilala Princess

Maleficent captures Kilala and Rei! If she wants to get free, Kilala will have to give up the magic tiara. If she refuses, Kilala will be forced to eat a poison apple—just like Snow White did! What will she choose?

JOIN KILALA AND THE DISNEY PRINCESSES FOR MORE ADVENTURES IN VOLUME 2!

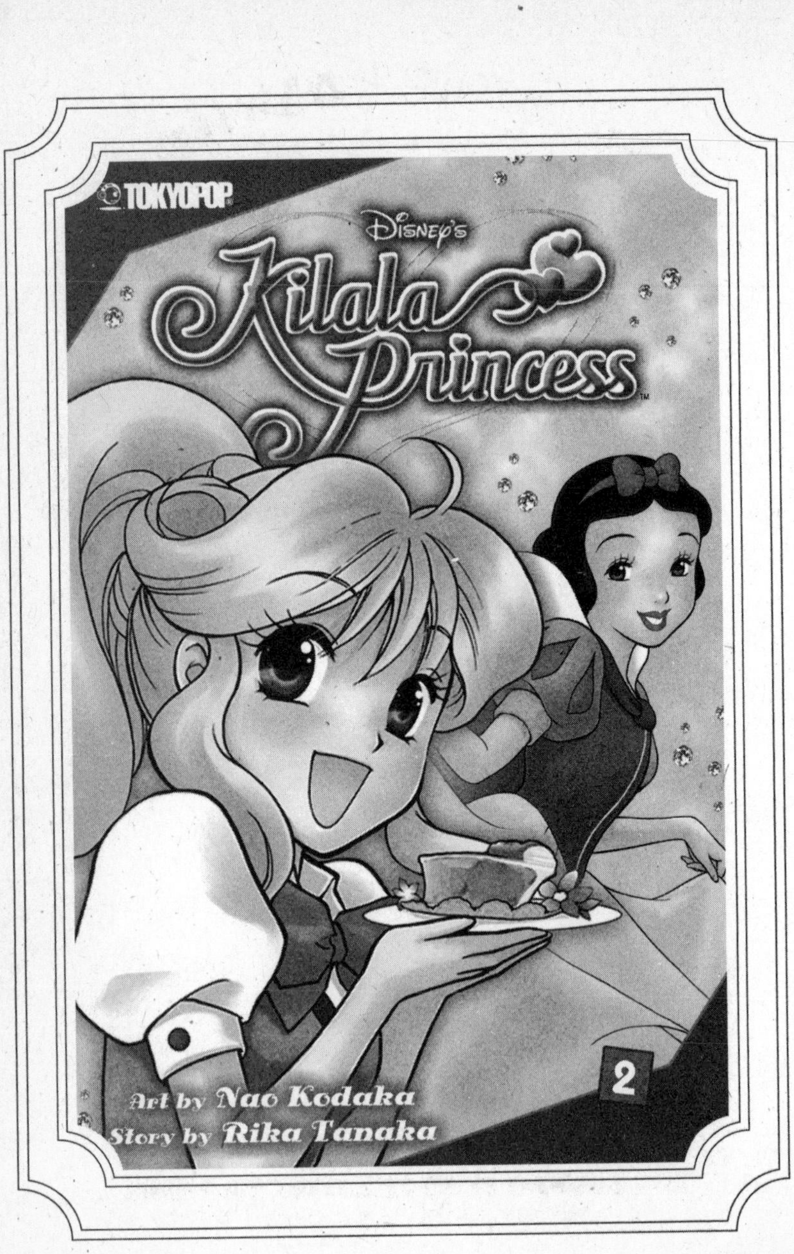
TOKYOPOP
DISNEY'S
Kilala Princess
2
Art by Nao Kodaka
Story by Rika Tanaka

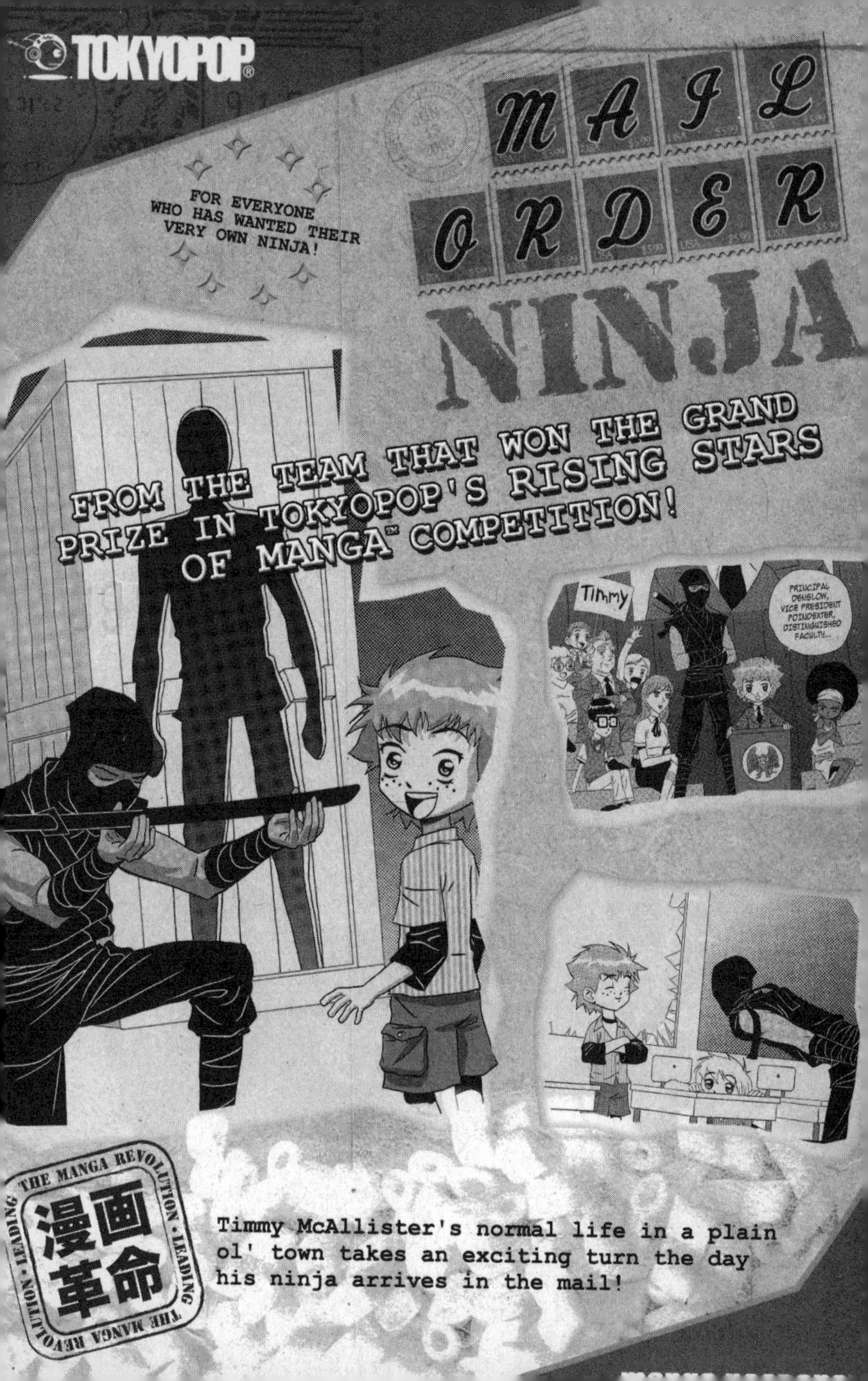
TOKYOPOP®
MAIL ORDER NINJA
FOR EVERYONE WHO HAS WANTED THEIR VERY OWN NINJA!
FROM THE TEAM THAT WON THE GRAND PRIZE IN TOKYOPOP'S RISING STARS OF MANGA™ COMPETITION!
Timmy
PRINCIPAL DENSLOW, VICE PRESIDENT POINDEXTER, DISTINGUISHED FACULTY...
THE MANGA REVOLUTION · LEADING THE MANGA REVOLUTION · LEADING
漫画革命
Timmy McAllister's normal life in a plain ol' town takes an exciting turn the day his ninja arrives in the mail!

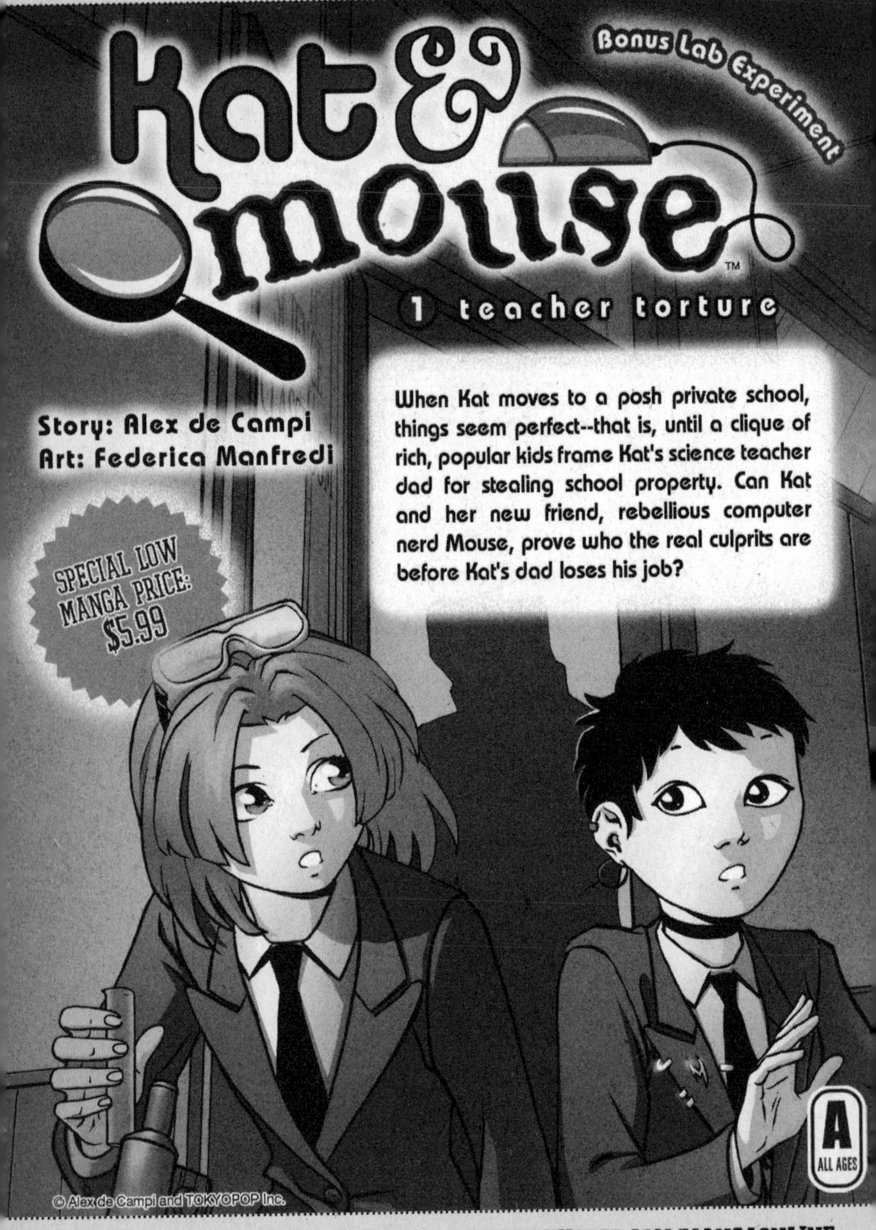
Kat & Mouse™
Bonus Lab Experiment
1 teacher torture
Story: Alex de Campi
Art: Federica Manfredi
When Kat moves to a posh private school, things seem perfect--that is, until a clique of rich, popular kids frame Kat's science teacher dad for stealing school property. Can Kat and her new friend, rebellious computer nerd Mouse, prove who the real culprits are before Kat's dad loses his job?
SPECIAL LOW MANGA PRICE: $5.99
A
ALL AGES
© Alex de Campi and TOKYOPOP Inc.

An All-New Movie On DISNEY DVD

Cinderella III: A Twist In Time

What If The Slipper Didn't Fit?

What If The Slipper Didn't Fit?

Find out more at Cinderella3DVD.com

STOP

THIS IS THE BACK OF THE BOOK!

How do you read manga-style? It's simple! To learn, just start in the top right panel and follow the numbers:

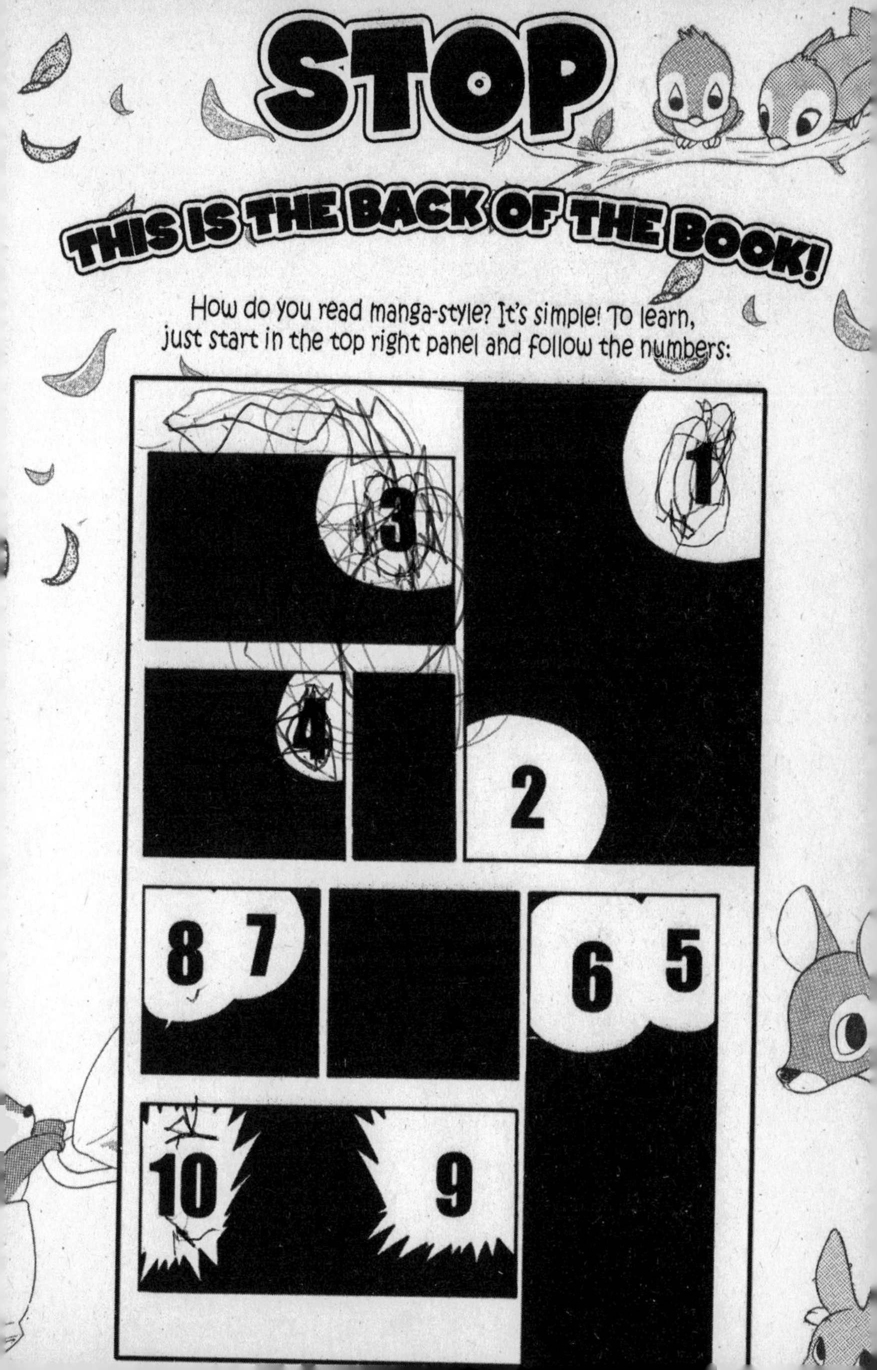
1
2
3
4
5
6
7
8
9
10

Kilala Princess Vol. 1
Written by Rika Tanaka
Illustrated by Nao Kodaka

English Adaptation - Kathy Schilling
Retouch and Lettering - Jennifer Carbajal
Graphic Designer - Monalisa De Asis

Editor - Hope Donovan
Digital Imaging Manager - Chris Buford
Pre-Production Supervisor - Erika Terriquez
Art Director - Anne Marie Horne
Production Manager - Elisabeth Brizzi
Managing Editor - Vy Nguyen
VP of Production - Ron Klamert
Editor-in-Chief - Rob Tokar
Publisher - Mike Kiley
President and C.O.O. - John Parker
C.E.O. and Chief Creative Officer - Stuart Levy

A **TOKYOPOP** Manga

TOKYOPOP Inc.
5900 Wilshire Blvd. Suite 2000
Los Angeles, CA 90036

E-mail: info@TOKYOPOP.com
Come visit us online at www.TOKYOPOP.com

ISBN: 978-1-59816-767-2

First TOKYOPOP printing: January 2007
10 9 8 7 6 5 4 3 2 1
Printed in the USA

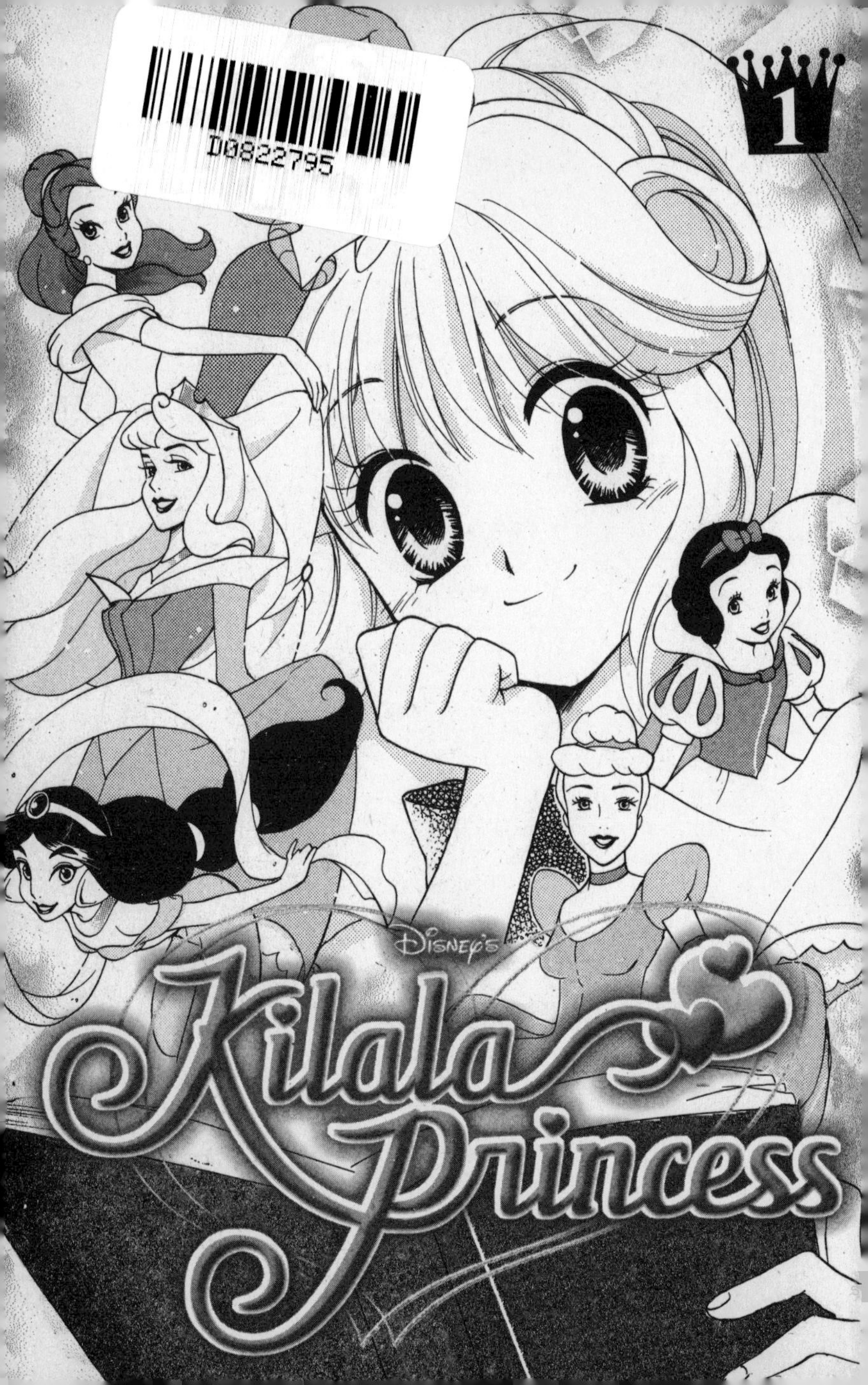
1
Disney's
Kilala Princess